Q-Art London is a free and open forum for students, graduates and self-trained artists. Q-Art runs regular crits – known as 'convenors' – in art colleges, artist studios and public gallery spaces as well as gallery tours, panel discussions and an end of year show. These events together with our publications aim to demystify often opaque art world discourses and make accessible the systems of art education and evaluation to current and wider audiences.

This is the second Q-Art publication.
Previous titles include:

12 Gallerists: 20 Questions
A Collection of Interviews with 12 London Gallerists.

Interviews for this publication gathered between April 2010 and April 2011.
Published in 2011 by Q-Art London ©
www.q-artlondon.com

ISBN: 978-0-9564355-1-4
Design by Jens Dan Johansen | www.jensdj.dk
Layout by Lars Rubæk Johansen

11 COURSE LEADERS: 20 QUESTIONS

A COLLECTION OF INTERVIEWS WITH
11 LONDON BA FINE ART COURSE LEADERS

CONTENTS

....

ACKNOWLEDGEMENTS

With thanks to the 11 Course Leaders who gave permission to reproduce their interviews in this publication. This project owes a lot to them and I thank them for their generosity both with their time and answers. Thank you also to Patricia Bickers for writing the Introduction and to Jo Allen, Andrew Bryant, Fiona Flynn, Jason Grant, Maggie Learmonth and Evelyn Wilson for their assistance and support.

NOTE

At the time of interview all of the tutors were in their respective positions. Some may have moved on since.

FOREWORD

By Sarah Rowles

The last two years have seen a proliferation of experimental art schools, panel discussions, publications and conversations all reflecting on what is perceived to be a current 'crisis' in UK undergraduate art education. At around the same time that much of this activity was beginning – or at least becoming more widely known – I entered the second year of my own BA Art Practice degree at Goldsmiths College, University of London. This was October 2008. In November of the same year, whilst I was still unaware of these conversations, I set up Q-Art London – an arts organisation that through events, debate, publications and online, strives to demystify the contemporary art world and undergraduate level art education.

My motivations for setting up Q-Art and for producing this book stem from my own path into and through art education and the observations and questions I developed along the way. Like many people in the UK with an interest in art, mine grew out of a childhood passion for drawing and making and for a good while it was my belief that the label 'art' was synonymous only with that which was figurative, decorative or highly-skilled. Art was what we could see by 'old masters' in the National Gallery, in small local museums and community centres, or in high street or sea front art shops by those working today.

It wasn't until the age of 18, when I moved to London, that I became aware of 'contemporary art', a genre in its own right. Contemporary art can be described as the type of work being made by artists who have usually been through undergraduate level art education, making work, wittingly or not, in response to a historical lineage of 'canonical' art. It may exist in any form, from painting, print, sculpture and video, to 'readymade' objects, installations and ideas, to a collaborative piece or performance. Contemporary art is that shown by the 300 plus contemporary art galleries that exist in London alone, as well as the similar numbers in other national and global centres, all inter-connected through an art market evaluation system which determines those works we will one day see in our national museums and galleries and those we will not.

At first sight, such work when you've not grown up to see it, not learnt the codes to read it, not safe in the knowledge that it's OK to *not* understand it – is intimidating. This unfamiliarity with contemporary art in the UK is what shuts many people out of it and is what in my view disadvantages many first year and 'first generation'[1] art students who have to spend much of their time silently playing 'catch up' with their peers who do have such experience and can cite the names of hundreds of artists from day one.

As a result of this, this book aims to do two things. The first is to go some way to illuminating how people with a similar background to my own, go from valuing the types of work widely recognised as art, to making and valuing contemporary art. The second, is to reveal the histories, mechanisms and philosophies of current undergraduate art education.

Art education deviates from a lot of other education, and the puzzles I just described becomes even more confusing when we are confronted by the common adage that art is a subject that 'cannot be taught'. Most fine art courses in the UK are 'broad-based' (non medium-specific), as is evidenced in the interviews that follow, and almost all do not have a set programme of practical tuition. They do not teach art history and have a preference for independent study. Are students expected to arrive with a knowledge of art history and a set of practical skills already in place? Are these things not important? Where exactly in art education does the education take place?

The interviews reveal a difference in approach between broad-based courses, those courses split into 'pathways' or modules, and those divided by discipline. Arguments are made for and against each approach and there are differences of opinion on appropriate levels of instruction. This in relation to crit dynamics, the handling of materials, art history and contact time, to mention but a few. Strong and persuasive cases are made by many of the course leaders for an education that prioritises individual discovery and self-realisation.

Asked about the apparent lack of in-depth practical skills tuition, course leaders cited the logistical and economic realities of teaching a growing student population the wide range of skills required to be an artist today. No course offers ongoing, timetabled instruction that will take a student through the various developmental stages of learning a 'craft', from 'novice to master'. Instead, courses provide introductory workshops on particular skills such as printmaking or casting at the beginning of the year, and/or instruction on a need-to-know basis. The course leaders were quick to point out that, because today artists may employ others to make things for them, work collaboratively, use 'readymades' and found objects, or produce work that is performance-based, participatory or social in nature, the refined acquisition of one particular skill wouldn't necessarily be of any use.

The structured academic study of art history is similarly lacking from the majority of courses and reasons given tend to parallel the above. To impose the idea that young artists must know the canon, and not only that but measure the value of their own creative activity against it, before they can even begin, is viewed as restrictive and oppressive. Students are encouraged to draw on references from art history and elsewhere that are relevant to their particular interests.

As the interviews progress it becomes clear that the current models of art education described above, have evolved through successive generations rethinking previous structures with the aim of improving upon their own experience. Educational philosophies in existence now were born in part from a desire to create a more liberating experience for current students. However, there is an abundance of literature, panel discussion and debate signaling the significant levels of dissatisfaction within art education, felt by students, tutors and artists. So why then, despite the good intentions of current course leaders and a desire for a more 'liberating' educational experience, is this the case?

Many commentators cite an aversion to risk taking amongst art students as symptomatic of this dissatisfaction. Students, who should be taking risks and experimenting – qualities commonly identified as crucial to art making – are instead agonising over justifying their creative decisions. Many think this is due to the bureaucratisation of art education brought about when art schools amalgamated with universities (something they had to do in order to survive). The effects of this include, in their terms: increased admin; over-academicisation of the subject; a new research and assessment culture; a preference for formal teaching qualifications; and increased student numbers impacting on space and resources. For these commentators art education was better before this change.

Contrary to my expectations however, many course leaders, whilst citing some of the frustrations these changes brought, were also at pains to tell me of their benefits. Many recall the unfair, overtly casual, cliquey and even sexist nature of their own art education and argue that the structures in place now allow for a better, fairer system. Those who have had teacher training note the invaluable gains, like proper report writing, negotiating group dynamics, leading crits and being aware of how to convey to a student what being an artist means. Some even argue that more structure, rather than less, allows students to feel more able to take risks.

Whilst the writing of a dissertation, a requirement of academic study, is often a point of contention, many argue that it provides the opportunity for deeper thought. Extended writing and research can for some open up a whole field of knowledge and engender a level of reflection otherwise undiscovered. On the whole, limited resources and smaller studio spaces due to increased numbers, are agreed to be a tolerable consequence of widening participation and access.

Course leaders cite other barriers to creative risk taking. To begin with, amongst students there is a widely perceived prioritisation of conceptual agendas over a more 'intuitive' materials or process-led approach to art making. This means students may try and resolve an idea before they begin making it, resulting in a limited amount of exploration. Secondly, there is a tendency for tutors to question students' choice of medium. Intended as a way to open up alternative approaches and solutions, this kind of intervention can be misconstrued as a challenge to students' values and beliefs, resulting in an inability to trust their own creative decisions.

So far I have focused on the internal, structural factors at play in the institutions of further and higher art education. But there is another element that looks set to have an overarching effect on the future of art education – and that is tuition fees.

All of the course leaders I interviewed received a free art education, plus a grant to live on. A week after I began the interviews, the Conservative-Liberal Democrat coalition government came into power. Despite numerous protests[2], recommendations made in a report by Lord Browne to raise tuition fees in England to a minimum of £6,000 and a maximum of £9,000 got approved by Parliament. By the time I'd completed the final interview, many of our top universities had already announced that they will be charging the full £9,000 for 2012 entry. The timescale of the election, the report, the announcements, and the protests are all charted in the interviews, which are arranged chronologically in this book.

With an increase in fees prospective students are likely to be more concerned about potential career opportunities. This means competition between courses will increase. As a result, unique selling points, such as reputation and specialist courses on offer will play a more significant role than they do already. There is a deep concern about the commoditisation of education and a fear among staff of students becoming positioned as 'customers' who can then turn around and say, "I want something better". The process of becoming an artist, many agree, requires that you are exposed to a certain amount of 'criticality' enabling you to become reflectively critical in your own practice. What will happen then if students reject this criticality and decide to take their money elsewhere? And what impact might this have on the way art courses operate?

My main aim for this book was to enable myself and others to get to grips with how and why art education has become what it is today as well as how an understanding of art as representational painting, drawing and sculpture can transform into an acceptance of and facility for, producing contemporary art.

Many students see the model of art education that they find themselves in, as natural or unconditioned, rather than the economically, politically and subjectively contingent institution that the interviews in this book reveal it to be. There are reasons why undergraduate art education is what it is and does what it does. It is my firm opinion that in uncovering and unpicking these reasons, students will be better situated to get a handle on what is happening to them, will feel more confident in their decision making and what they choose to practice, and be better equipped to steer a course through.

Without doubt, the culture of the various teaching institutions in which new students immerse themselves, is instrumental in shaping the artists that later emerge. The problem is that these cultures, and the wider forces that influence them, stay mostly hidden. What do remain visible, tend to be the more seductive influences, like art market preferences and college reputations. Students need to be aware of all of these influences in order that they can make informed decisions as to what they take on board and what they reject.

There is something else to bear in mind too. The course leaders to whom this book is indebted were once undergraduate students themselves. Their experience was very different to the experience of my generation. Art education has changed, it will change again, and the origins of that change will come – as always – from those in it now.

1   This is a term used within higher education to describe students who are the first in their family to go to university.

2   The Conservative-Liberal Democrat coalition government came into power on May 12th 2010. On October 12th 2010 Lord Browne's review of higher education funding in England was published. On November 3rd 2010 universities minister, David Willetts announced proposals to raise tuition fees to between £6,000 and £9,000. On November 10th 2010 the first major student protest over tuition fees occurred, focussed in London. On November 24th and December 9th 2010 student protests took place across the UK. On December 9th 2010 the bill to raise tuition fees to a minimum of £6,000 was passed by a majority of 21 votes.

INTRODUCTION

By Patricia Bickers, Editor of Art Monthly

"It's not like it used to be when I was a student. Thank God!"

Mo Throp was referring to her days as a student at St. Martin's, as it then was, but her comment is echoed by many others who went to art school in 'the good old days'. Speaking at an *Art Monthly* panel discussion on art education in 2008, 40 years after the student uprisings in Paris, London and elsewhere in 1968, Phyllida Barlow for instance remembered the casual sexism, the macho culture and the unapologetic elitism of art schools in the sixties whose staff and students were overwhelmingly white and middle class.[1] Not much changed in the 1970s and eighties – or even nineties. Rosemarie McGoldrick recalls that, though the ratio of staff to student at Chelsea was virtually 1:1 – a ratio that seems scarcely credible today (Andrew Bannister boasts lower-than-average staff student ratios at City and Guilds which is, of course, still independent), she hardly ever saw any of her tutors in any case because they were always "down the pub".

Power, as Throp was only too aware, was not in the hands of students, especially not female students and, despite the fact that they were often in the majority, as at St. Martins when Throp was studying there, female students were often given less attention as artists than their male counterparts (and sometimes rather too much attention in other respects). In terms of staff, the very opposite was the case. In McGoldrick's time at Chelsea there were no female tutors at all while Dereck Harris points out that, even in the early eighties when he was a student, the staff was "pretty much an exclusively male team". In terms of student satisfaction, there would appear to be something of a gender divide in these recollections, however Stephen

Carter also complains of the "egotistical" and "opinionated" teaching that he experienced as a student in the eighties, especially during 'crits', while Martin Newth believes that the student experience today is generally better than his own at Newcastle. And while, as Louis Nixon points out, the crit – along with the tutorial, seminar and artist talk – is still a standard feature of fine art teaching in the UK, all those interviewed now favour a less confrontational approach – even, according to Michael Archer, in the case of the notorious 'convenors' at Goldsmiths.

Back then, concepts such as 'student satisfaction' and 'student centred learning' were not part of the vocabulary of art or any other form of education, while surveys to measure student satisfaction, a standard exercise in most art departments and colleges today, would then have been seen as a totally unnecessary imposition. On the contrary it could be said that staff satisfaction was the chief concern. John Aiken points out, for instance, that in the sixties and seventies teaching in art schools was seen primarily as "a mechanism for supporting artists". How times change. A recent research paper titled *The Changing Face of Artists' Employment* showed that, while teaching within the further and higher education sector represents a third of all work available to artists which, overall, has dropped by half since the recession of 2008, it predicted that such jobs are likely to be drastically reduced in the wake of the government's decision to abolish all funding for the arts and humanities.[2] In fact jobs in art education are already being cut.

In any case, since the introduction of fees, the balance of power has shifted from staff to students – those who can afford to go to university in the first place, that is, or who are willing to shoulder the burden of debt that they will incur as a result of the coalition government's decision to implement the recommendations of Lord Browne's report and raise fees to a maximum of £9,000 a year.[3] This was a dilemma that none of those interviewed had to face, as they candidly admit in response to Sarah Rowles's gentle probing. Whereas education used to be free for the majority, fewer people actually went to college or university. In contrast, the success of New Labour's policies of 'social inclusion' and 'widening participation' has meant that there has been a vast increase in the percentage of people going into further and higher education generally, and from ethnic minorities and low income families in particular. Of course this success is now being undermined by the imposition of fees, ironically a policy that New Labour also introduced.

Consumer power is, of course, a travesty of the kind of political power demanded by the *Les Soixante-Huitards*,[4] some of whom demanded nothing less than a revolution – political, social and educational. If there has been a revolution in recent years, it has arguably been a conservative one – in both senses. When, at a stroke, Conservative Prime Minister Margaret Thatcher turned polytechnics into universities in 1992, it was less about raising their status – though that is how many in art education chose to see it at the time – than about homogenising education provision and reducing the autonomy of art colleges. The result was an outbreak of 'merger mania', as formerly independent art schools merged to form larger institutions, or were absorbed by the new universities. Rowles's decision to undertake this survey is timely, given that many of the interviews took place against the backdrop of student protest against the fee increases, and sit-ins in protest at, for instance, the merger between Byam Shaw and Central Saint Martins. Paradoxically, though there are now, as Harris points out, more fine art courses on offer in the UK per capita than anywhere else in the world, as a result of this process of homogenisation, which also extends to the modularised curriculum, there is, as Newth ruefully acknowledges, a certain "sameness" across institutions.

So much for the idea of 'consumer choice' that is so dear to politicians of whatever stripe. Nevertheless, there is no lack of competition between institutions, particularly in London. On the contrary, competition is especially fierce in the race to recruit full fee-paying international students – education is now a major business, one that is increasingly run after the US model. McGoldrick is open about her concern, magnified by a recent conversation with a colleague in New York, that high fees could put critical rigour at risk and compromise the relationship between staff and student, turning staff into what Dean Kenning has described as mere 'service providers', rather than teachers.[5] McGoldrick is not alone in trying to resist

21

on the one hand the marketisation of art education and the encroachment – Stephen Lee[6] has described it as the 'colonisation' of one culture by another – of corporate language, talk of 'learner outcomes' and 'transferable skills' etc, and on the other the threat of professionalisation and academicisation. John Timberlake, for example, is forthright in championing the "radical uselessness" of art against the growing instrumentalist approach to art education within institutions. It is ironic that the pressure to perform well in the government imposed RAE (Research Assessment Exercise, now the REF, Research Excellence Framework) together with the requirement for teaching qualifications and the proliferation of what Throp amusingly refers to as "Ph-bloody-Ds" in fine art (despite having both herself) would have excluded many of the most influential artist/teachers in the past – from John Baldessari to Martha Rosler, Mary Kelly to John Latham – from teaching at all.

But then they didn't in fact teach, since the consensus then and even to a great extent now, is that fine art can't be taught. Instead for Newth the aim is to provide "the circumstances whereby students can learn" and the "space" for "possibilities" to occur. Similarly for Nixon it is about "setting up an environment for something creative to happen". Jane Lee concurs, but adds: "We creatively and constructively intervene in a student's practice. Art education is essentially that intervention into someone's practice." "Art teachers don't make artists", Timberlake insists, "art teachers provide an education to give people the *opportunity* to learn to become artists." Michael Archer, too, prefers the word "educate" to "teach" and, returning to the root of the verb which is "to lead out of …", describes an art education as "a process" that enables "what is already there in the students to find a way out".

Long may they all continue to *not* teach art.

1 'What is the Future of Art Education?'
   Part 2, Ikon Gallery, October 6, 2008.
   Panel members were: Phyllida Barlow,
   Pavel Büchler, Michael Corris and
   Vaughan Grylls, chaired by Patricia
   Bickers. http://www.artmonthly.co.
   uk/magazine/site/events/category/
   roadshow/

2 *The Changing Face of Artists' Employment'* published by The Artists Information Company, May 2011.

3 Lord Browne's Report's recommendations on raising tuition fees were
   accepted by coalition Government
   on Dec 9, 2010.

4 'Les Soixante Huitards', or 'The 68ers',
   refers to the generation of students and
   strikers who took part in protests in
   Paris, London and elsewhere in 1968.

5 Dean Kenning 'Protest. Occupy.
   Transform', *Art Monthly,* No. 343
   February 2011, pp. 34-5.

6 'When one culture colonises another
   it imposes its jargon by replacing the
   existing culture's language with its
   own.' Letters *Art Monthly* No. 316,
   May 2008.

JOHN TIMBERLAKE

John Timberlake is programme leader for
the BA Fine Art course at Middlesex University.
This interview took place in John's office in late April 2010.

How long have you been teaching on this course for?
I've been programme leader here since 2007, so not very long. Before that I was Subject Leader at the University of Wolverhampton in the photography department and I also contributed towards the MA Fine Art and MA Photography teaching there. I've been teaching in higher education for twelve years now in various Art and Design subjects.

What makes you switch from place to place?
Just career opportunities. If jobs come up in places I want to work seem attractive and suit my agenda as an artist, I apply for them.

Did you study art yourself?
Yes.

Where was that?
First off I did a foundation course near my hometown. Then I did my BA at Brighton Polytechnic, which is now the University of Brighton. I did the Fine Art Alternative Practice BA, which is now Fine Art Critical Practice. After that I did a teaching certificate in teaching fine art at post-compulsory education level at Greenwich University. It's what's called PCET: Post Compulsory Education Training. I also did the Whit-

ney Independent Study Studio Programme at the Whitney Museum of American Art in New York.

What's that?
It's the Whitney Programme. If you don't know what that is it's your problem! That's a bit like saying, "What's Goldsmiths?" or something!

(Both laugh)

The Whitney Museum of American Art runs an independent studio programme, which is open for artists and curators to apply for. You spend a year there with a studio space in Manhattan. I won a bursary to do so.

Wow. Oh I think I have read about it, is it the place where the likes of Andrea Fraser and Mark Dion studied?
Yes, they have an incredible list of people. Those you mention are the 'young blood' but they also have Gayatri Spivak, Martha Rosler, Hans Haacke, Fred Wilson, Isaac Julien, Benjamin Buchloh, Hal Foster, Mary Kelly and so on. It's an amazing roster of faculty.

As a result of that I've never technically done a Masters. My postgraduate study was a combination of showing work in London, working on *Everything* magazine, subsequent further study and so on. I wasn't someone who just went straight from a BA to an MA as some people have done in the past.

What was it you said you did at Greenwich?
PGCE (FE), which qualifies me to teach in further and higher education, but not in schools.

Does everyone have to have one of those to teach at HE level?
Institutions are encouraging it and they like it if you do. If you don't have one at the point of acceptance they generally require that you do one.

A lot of people are reflecting on a time when artists 'just taught' art courses and did not have to be trained as teachers ...
That is true, however, I personally take the view that a teaching certificate is a good thing. I was an artist before I did my teacher training thing, but I actually think that the training aspect of the certificate helped me. I do think that it does make better lecturers, particularly given the pressures these days on anyone teaching at any level.

Can you give an example of how it helps?
Yes, OK. In terms of managing numbers, for example, when I did my degree I was in a year group of eight students within Fine Art Alternative Practice. I wouldn't have thought there were more than 40 across the entire year of sculpture, painting and print. Today we have situations where there can be, say, seventy students in a year – we have 60 this year – and that places different demands on tutors. For example, the Wolverhampton photography course that I used to lead entailed a lot of instruction. Lots of expositional teaching had to be done. So if you're in a classroom for three hours, or if you're in a studio, a dark room or a digital suite showing a class how to do something, you need the ability to understand how that works. You need to be able to manage a class and the learning process, and if you haven't had any training it's very stressful. The idea that you can just 'be an artist' without thinking reflectively about how you will communicate what that means in a classroom or group situation in the studio would be naïve, and lead to lots of disgruntled students.

On one level it's important that teachers of art model professionalism as an artist. In order to teach art I think it's important that you *are* an artist. How that works in a teaching situation is that you need to have a cognitive understanding of the processes of making art, but also the processes by which different people learn, and those understandings have to be tested.

Pedagogically I'd identify myself as a Vygotskian. Lev Vygotsky was an early Soviet era educationalist. I don't know how many tutors could actually put a name to their methodology of teaching but I think it's important that you can and that you can make decisions and rationalise your choices of teaching according to a clear set of concerns.

What made you decide to teach?
I wanted to improve myself as an artist and I wanted a channel for my artistic interests and engagements that went beyond simply making work and showing it. When I left college I got a First Class Honours with Commendation from Brighton, but despite that I decided not to do an MA at that stage. Financially I couldn't afford it and my parents couldn't support it. My parents are from a working class background and it had been a big strain for them to support me as a student on the BA.

I decided to stay in Brighton for a while but a lot of people who I was at college with tended to melt away quite quickly, so I ended up feeling quite isolated, in a town without familial support. I did a series of jobs that were totally unrelated to art and that put a pressure on the time I had for art practice. Nevertheless, I carried on doing solo and group shows post-graduation, both in Brighton and then when I moved to London.

A conflict which I think lots of young artists without financial security face is making art whilst holding down a job that pays the rent. That situation can make it difficult to focus. So there came a point where I needed to look towards getting a post in a college.

By that time I'd been working for several years in homeless hostel work, which suited me in a lot of ways and built up my people skills in terms of dealing with and working with young people. The experience also made me aware of older people who were perhaps on a learning curve as it was the first time I'd really thought of people in their fifties still learning. I learnt a lot working with drug dependency workers, alcohol dependency workers, social workers...and I came to think that education was related to that in some way and that I would have the skills and aptitude to do it. So I applied to Greenwich University to do the Fine Art PGCE (FE) and they accepted me.

Do you have a specialist area that you teach in?
This course is a broad range course. We don't have separate sub-programmes of, say, printmaking or painting – like, for example, Wimbledon.

Saying that, within the cohort of staff there *are* different specialisms. In the past ten to twelve years my own practice has focussed principally on painting, drawing and photography, and so those tend to be the areas I specialise in, in terms of teaching. But all of us have tutor groups that include people who have interests in other areas, and we teach across them.

I have also had some experience of collaborative practices, partly because it was a common modus operandi in London in the 1990s.

I did some work with groups like BANK and I also worked on *Everything* magazine as part of the editorial collective. I worked on that from 1994 until the magazine's demise in 2002.

So my practice for quite a while was textual and I do write. I wrote recently for *Radical Philosophy* and I have produced fiction and other texts that have been published. I don't write reviews for art magazines, though, because it doesn't interest me to do that.

I also did a performance piece for BANK in '96 and then at the ICA in '98. In terms of my background there have been a range of overlapping concerns and experiences spanning across different forms of my practice. They all inform my teaching, beyond the particular concerns I have now.

Do you think the practice of the tutors have any influence on the work that the students make?
Inevitably mimesis does play a role, but that doesn't imply some sort of duplication. Tutors work hard to try and make sure that that doesn't happen.

I mean if you're an artist you don't want a group of clones! You tend to want to push people in other directions and you can be generous and supportive of a student in doing that. Sometimes their work has been pushed into directions you haven't been able to follow yourself but that you find interesting – and that's one of the delights of teaching.

We've been speaking about teaching; do you think art can be taught?
The key thing about teaching – and I was taught this by my tutor at teacher training and fully subscribe to it – is that ultimately teaching is about creating a situation in which learning can take place. How do people learn? Well, often it's by making mistakes. I believe art teaching always has a strong heuristic aspect.

It's not simply about expositional instruction. Of course, techniques, in and of themselves, can be taught. You can tell someone to put that normally exposed film in a Paterson tank and to agitate it every 30 seconds for eight minutes at 20 degrees centigrade, or tell them to overexpose it and leave it in for only six minutes and 24 seconds. You can also tell somebody how to prepare a canvas or use a colour wheel. But if you're asking, "Can *art* be taught?" I'd say the key thing is about creating a situation in which people feel free – psychologically safe, in other words – to show the results, whether good or bad, and reflect and talk about what they've done in a range of situations, and to be able to distinguish between what they wanted to do and what they've *actually* done in a constructive way. A mistake or a failure seen with fresh eyes, suddenly becomes interesting.

Some institutions do this well and others fail very, very badly. That's why you get students who come out of institutions feeling chewed up, bitter, upset and whatever. It's not rocket science but it does seem to elude some people. Some people think that the way to teach is to hector or to tear apart. I don't subscribe to that and that's not been my ethos in my time here or at any other place.

So how do you create that environment?

You let people feel comfortable, feel secure, and feel supported. It's important to create a situation where students feel able to talk to other students. So you don't allow situations where cliques or bullying can take place. One of the key ways you do that as a tutor is by modelling a humane, appreciative, supportive approach to work via inclusive conversations. Obviously some students are going to be a lot better than other students but it doesn't alter the fact that good teaching works at any level. If a teacher knows what they are doing and knows their craft then a teacher can teach any age range.

What forms of teaching do you have here?

There are crits, group tutorials, one-to-one tutorials, seminars, visiting fine art lecturers, presentations by students; and then there is committee work where students prepare catalogues etc for the final degree show. I know compared to other institutions we seem to have a lot of contact time.

How does the crit work here?

We have a series of presentations. For example, in the second year, students present their work through the lens of what they're interested in, rather than presenting on the objects themselves. That's then supplemented by individual tutorial sessions. In group tutorials we might spend a day or an afternoon with ten students going around their spaces.

How does your critical studies programme work?

We have a team who teach from their own specialities. Jean Fisher for example is here and delivers lectures on Transcultural studies and Globalisation. Jon Bird does a series of lectures about Modernism and its development, whilst Stewart Martin and Luke White, two young and very capable thinkers, do lectures on aspects of art history, philosophy and critical theory.

We also have visiting lecturers, practitioners and curators who are asked to address a particular problematic in as broad a way as they see fit.

Do you think students who enter art school having grown up seeing art are at more of an advantage when making and reading work?
I think it's about aptitude for learning more than prior knowledge. If someone's open to learning at the point at which they enter college, it's possible that they don't have to have a substantial amount of previous knowledge. What they must do is demonstrate potential in their portfolio and demonstrate a critical awareness.

Inevitably some students feel more confident being in an art environment than others. If, for the sake of argument, your mother and father were both successful artists, the condition of studying art that you find yourself in at 21 or whatever is going to be naturalised to you in the same way that you don't think twice about the taps in your mother's bathroom, you just turn them on. If on the other hand you've never experienced those kinds of fixtures and fittings then you obviously need time to acclimatise!

(Both laugh)

Inevitably what we look for at interview is both a commitment and also an understanding of what fine art is. We were interviewing yesterday and we turned down quite a few, many of who had promising work, but clearly demonstrated during the course of the interview that they didn't know *why* their work was art and not say, graphic design or illustration. Others don't have the intellectual, written or visual skills to thrive on the course. There are some people who don't have any idea what it is to be an artist.

How does someone get that idea?
There's no single narrative. Looking back to when I worked in the homeless hostels one of the first things they'd ask you at interview was, "How

do people become homeless?" It's a trick question. If you say, "It's because people become alcoholics," or, "because people lose their jobs, their spouses leave them and they enter a tragic spiral of decline and dereliction," then you're falling prey to popular prejudices. The reasons people become homeless are million-fold, in the same way that the reasons why someone might have a good aptitude for art school are million-fold. The reason *why* doesn't matter. It would if we were some fifth or sixth generation Bloomsbury set or something, where it was about 'people like us' who come from the 'right background' and have 'the right family connections' or have done the right things socially, but it's not. It's not a debutants' ball.

The key thing is that someone can demonstrate they have the willingness, aptitude and basic skills to develop on a fine art course. At interview, I'd rather see a portfolio of interesting mistakes than boring successes.

I think that foundation courses are really good because they ground people in knowing what they do want to do. If someone has explored lots of different things on their foundation course and then gets onto the BA course and decides they only want to paint red roses, that's fine as they've tried all those other things out first. But if someone comes straight from A-Level and decides all they want to paint is red roses then they're not going to get onto this course.

I'm exaggerating to make the point.

It worked.
And if foundation courses were to disappear then the pressure to go through that development stage gets pushed into the first year of higher education – and that's something we have to resist.

They're not disappearing though are they?
I hope not. But there have been changes in what kind of courses are on offer, and we seem to get a relatively large number of applicants who think they can forego doing foundation study.

Did you yourself grow up seeing art?

My parents had no conception of how I could be an artist but they spotted early on that I had an aptitude for art. But it's going back to the psychology of why any of us want to do it in the end. I wanted to be an artist once I stopped wanting to be an astronaut – very young.

I always drew and made things out of Plasticine and I always wanted to paint and draw. I did it all the way through my teens too, it was a compulsion. Even though my parents didn't have much of an understanding of art they always supported me. My dad was an engineer and he worked 41 years in the same engineering factory.

I'd always been fascinated by engineering but he was adamant that he didn't want me to go into it. I think he saw my interest in art as a way for me to escape 'factory life' and so he encouraged it, even though he freely admitted that at times he didn't understand what I was doing. I've always been grateful for that. My parents wanted me to be free of the lives they'd had to lead and they believed in education as a way of doing that. I think all good parents, ultimately, want their children to be free of them. My mother always took me to see exhibitions and she'd buy me books on art. It was that thing of trying to find a way, even though it was a thing that they had no clue about. I grew up in a small town in east Lancashire in the 1970s and 80s. The world of contemporary art was a long way off.

I'm fascinated by the switch that occurs when many of us enter further and higher education to study art. The codes and values of art that many of us held and shared with our parents – say for example of craft and life-like representation – somehow have to change when we enter the world of contemporary art. And despite all the educational reasons given for it … I still feel a little uncomfortable, even guilty.

I became aware of contemporary art quite late on, when I was on my foundation course. There was a TV programme called *State of the Art* that was produced by Sandy Nairne. It had some interviews with big artists from the eighties and it was a real eye-opener. I think the first time I saw the Turner Prize was in 1986 on a foundation course trip to London – the one Derek Jarman and Art & Language (A&L) were in. I was appalled and intrigued, but I have to say I don't feel guilty in the way I think you're describing. I learned, quite quickly, to pick through what was interesting and useful in relation to both Jarman and A&L.

As parents we bear our children on our shoulders for a purpose – so that in time they have a chance of doing and seeing things differently than we can. So it was with ours. If they could see all that we can, they'd have been able to do it themselves. That's what necessitates history.

Do you think it's important for students to see the work of the staff?
Not particularly, but I do think it's important that students know that staff make art and have experienced what it means to be an artist. The first reason I think it's important is because I think that engagement with art should be an on going thing and that your skill sets and presumptions have to be challenged all the time. The second reason is because I think it is important to see a modelled account of being an artist in the studio. My position is that it's important that staff model a professional practice so that students can be aware of that and model themselves for or against that way of working through that process. Artists do not have a set career path in the way a dentist or a doctor does and so I think the more living examples you can provide, the better.

I also think it's important because it keeps us grounded as academics. I have my successes and failures as an artist and that makes me a better teacher. With knowledge of funding, availability of spaces, opportunities etc, I'm also aware of what is and isn't possible, and what it's like 'out there'. That places me ahead of the students but not too far ahead, and that's a good place to teach from. That's within what Lev Vygotsky calls the 'Zones of Proximal Development' or ZPDs. Part of learning is about identifying achievable goals for yourself. This is something that happens in key working in homeless hostels. A key worker sits down with the client and together they identify and set goals that will stretch that person, but which aren't unobtainable to the point where the person becomes demoralised.

I am doing a PhD at Goldsmiths and I posed a seminar model for the PhD, which was subsequently adopted. It was based on Systemic Therapy. They had got into a method of picking apart individuals with a silent audience, i.e. one person aggressively attacks a student researcher whilst the audience remains silent, except for the occasionally rather chilly comments coming in from the fringes.

We eventually had a seminar about seminars and I proposed that we abandon that model for one that promoted a sympathetic conversation between the interlocutor and the researcher. So in other words, the research student presenting selects someone they can have a sustained and humane conversation with. They then remain silent whilst the group has a conversation about the conversation. So it's a cascading, tiered approach.

I have been told by staff and students that the model is a success.

Can you go into a bit more detail?
OK. So you've got to stay silent whilst other people talk about what they did and didn't understand about your conversation. So for example, if you and I had a long conversation about this table …

(Points to table we are sitting at)

… and we didn't mention that it is made out of chipboard; when the other people have the conversation and mention that it was made out of chipboard, I can't then turn around and say, "Oh, I was going to say that, of course I knew it was chipboard!" You've got to be quiet. The key thing there in the feedback is that you've overlooked the blindingly obvious and that needs to be accounted for. That's a good thing. It's often the case that otherwise we miss something that should be fundamental to the discussion.

So I think there are analogies. I'm not saying art teaching is therapy but there are points where – like in the creation of a safe environment or identifying attainable goals – they can be compared. I set myself goals now as an artist: where I want to be in five years and the kind of space I want to be showing in etc.

So you learnt these pedagogical models from …
Teacher training. That is why I think it is important and should be taken seriously. I also learnt from having spent nine years working in homeless hostels and watching how professionals in the field helped those people. And I got into conversations with them about their techniques and approaches.

A classic example is that I remember once having a conversation about alcohol abuse. It was a meeting for staff about alcohol and the lady running it began the discussion by asking us how much we drank. That immediately created a situation where we realised alcoholism is a sliding scale and that you can quickly become embroiled in it. And it's the same with art. David Risley [a gallerist] once said to me, "Art's an addiction." He meant it flippantly, but in a sense it *is* true. And it helps that we too are involved in the same struggles, at some level, that our students are.

The trick is to maintain that level in a way that is somehow useful. It has to be formalised, it has to be disciplined. We can't all just collapse into a big emotional heap of self-pity. We have to think about ways that we can use our experience as teachers to benefit students in a positive way.

Because of my age I am only familiar with the current art educational system and not the old one. Can I ask you to compare art education now to how it was when you studied at art school? Were practical skills taught then? Were the changes made in approaches to teaching a result of ideology or economics?
I think it varied from course to course but I wasn't taught a core set of skills; skills were made available to me on the basis of a request and as a student I sought out the skills I decided I needed. For example, I remember that I became fascinated by book binding for a while and so I sought that out.

There were also some basic craft inductions: video editing, photography and so on. But I think generally fine art skills are dispensed on a need to know basis. You can't possibly sit students down and teach them all the skills they might ever want as an artist; the idea of that is preposterous! A ten-year, full-time course would not do that! You can't teach art in that way.

I genuinely do think that students I teach get a better and more full taught component than I did and I could cite examples but I won't. I think modularisation has helped and nearly all colleges now have some form of modularised component, whether they call it that or not. Numbers are greater and that's one of the reasons it needed to happen. I'm not sure that it is not without its problems but there are certain named components to the course with named outcomes and assessable points, and that has changed things.

But the classic example of change is curating. I wasn't taught anything about that. Twenty years ago, saying you were a freelance curator was relatively rare as curators were primarily attached to institutions. Now though, over the last 15 to 20 years we've seen the rise in this phenomenon of the curator. I've written about how I think that was a managerialism that rose on the back of artists who independently organised shows. If you look at the early nineties there wasn't this preponderance of curators, so it was more a case of groups of artists organising themselves. After a certain point the 'DJ's d'art' came in and started doing stuff. Mixing. And I have real problems with that. I've turned down shows on occasions because I thought the DJ aspect was too high and that it flattened down the work. But you do have these large numbers now of freelance curators and that does affect the way artists view the art world.

In terms of whether the changes in teaching are ideological or economic, I'd argue that the two are not so easily separated. Take for example student expectations, something you might say are purely ideological. How students view a course is bound to change if they are paying fees for it. And if their parents are paying the fees then that will affect the relationship between the student and the parent, i.e. family life. I think students living at home have a very different relationship with their parents than I had with mine whilst I was studying and living away from home. It's a matter of economic independence.

The problem we've got now is that tertiary education is more grounded in the domestic and the family home than it has been at any other point in recent history. I think that does create a parental scrutiny of art and of student life that inevitably leads to less freedom on the part of the student. I think that and things like student debt, are also why students are less likely to feel able to take risks than they might otherwise be.

On some courses you also get parents who complain because they think they're not getting their money's worth – even if their son or daughter is a failing student. As a result, this can quite often lead to a certain pressure to teach and learn quantifiable things. Yet in the face of our predominantly utilitarian culture, I think art, at its best, is radically useless. The radical quality of art is that it has *no* use in a culture that is dominated by profit, loss and use value. So it's always going to fly in the face of people if art can't account for itself. Those things always weigh heavily in art education and demonstrate the interrelationship of economics and ideology. This is not an argument to dispense with art education or to question its viability. Rather, I'm arguing it needs to be robustly defended on its own terms.

Do you think students should be taught professional skills?
We have a series of lectures and discussions around the art world as how it is constituted, and looking at different approaches to that.

We don't have a separate course for personal and professional development. That's not because I'm not against it, in fact I think there's a strong case for it. But the key point perhaps to flag up here is the need to prepare students as artists and also prepare them for the 'art world' as a social milieu.

The art world can seriously screw you up. People are often incredibly rude in the art world. I was always under the impression that the middle classes were a lot more polite and cultured. Well they might be cultured but they're certainly not more polite. My own experience of the London art world also became an awareness of just how vulgar and uncouth privilege can make people. So in that sense, you need to be able to train artists to be able to deal professionally with that sort of thing and to not get hurt personally. Unfortunately I also think that those kinds of things can also be reflected in educational institutions and there are institutions that do mess people up. The worst examples of art teaching in the past have created cliques and exclusions and have seriously damaged people, showing no sense of moral responsibility. Inevitably, in an environment as filled with clamour as the art world, there are some people who are horrible snobs and a dysfunctional approach to art education can contribute towards the conventions and mechanisms that promulgate that.

So teaching 'professional skills' in my view should be about teaching techniques like hanging, presentation etc. It's also got to prepare students for the worst, i.e. for things like dealing with rejection or carrying on working when no one seems to be noticing. It's no use just saying, "I'm the artist and people will learn from me," without properly thinking through the process of teaching these issues. It has to be a cognitive process and things have to be named, described and talked about.

But should students, whilst they are studying, be kept in that learning bubble and away from knowledge about how galleries and the Arts Council and so on works?
I think you've got to let people know their chances. You can't give them an illusion. You've got to let them know that the skills and opportunities that art creates may not be realised in a lifetime, however many superstars seem to be instantly made.

The skills that go into making you an artist are skills that should be valued by society. They mainly aren't but they should be. Artists should themselves be aware of those values.

What are the values?
Things like speaking up for yourself; like independence; responsibility. Having a strong sense of self and a realistic sense of self is vital to health. A lot of the students who do art will not become artists but I don't want

those students to feel that their time was wasted. The skills are transferable. The skills I applied in my homeless hostel work, and other walks of life, I owe in part to my art education.

They are transferable and a lot of people say that about art education. But if students do actually go on to do something other than follow a career as an artist, do you not think that they're made to feel a bit guilty? I'm talking I guess about if that decision is made whilst the student is still at art school. Assessments don't allow for that kind of change in direction do they?
I wouldn't want someone to feel guilty if they decide they didn't want to be an artist. I'd want them to feel that they gained skills and possibilities through being on an art course. And that's what an art education is. An art education isn't about manufacturing an artist.

But the course can only assess for artists?
Of course. You wouldn't give someone a first just because they have great interpersonal skills! I wouldn't say that for a minute. I'm not marking on the basis that they'd make a good middle manager. I'm assessing their work as a fine art student – with an emphasis on 'student' as well as 'fine art'.

But that's not the whole issue is it? Take this example:
Person A leaves college in 2006 with a first. However she does not immediately get snapped up by the Lisson Gallery or whatever. Ten years on she has a child, a job and she remembers that thing inside of her that she had when she was doing art and decides that she wants to do it again. That's a real life situation and a story of someone who has got the skills from that education and has had to apply them to other walks of life.

Art education has to serve the purposes of art *education* in the same way as say, an art magazine has to serve the purposes of being an art *magazine*. Neither is art itself. Art teachers don't make artists; art teachers provide an education to give people the opportunity to learn to become artists.

That's a fascinating answer, thank you.

Changing the subject slightly, can I move on to talk about the transition that saw all art colleges switch from being colleges to universities …
Yes, post-1992 was when art colleges all became universities.

Yes. Do you think anything was lost as a result of that? Or gained for that matter?
I don't know because I was the last generation of art students to go through a polytechnic system before it changed. Personally I don't think it really matters.

I think a far more fundamental change happened in 1990 when housing benefits stopped for students. I know this sounds really banal and humdrum but that is actually far more important. The simple fact is that had housing benefit not been available to me, it would have been a lot harder for me to go through art education and certainly to do it in Brighton. And the thing about Brighton was that it was about as far away from my hometown as I could get! That was deliberate. I grew up in Burnley and I just wanted to get out.

If I hadn't had that my whole experience of education would have been different and it would have also posed a different dynamic between me and my parents. That goes back to my earlier point. To give you one example, I had a difficult second year as a student. My work was changing and I couldn't think what to do. We've all had it; it's like writers block. I told my mum when she came down to see me and I said, "I've done no work, I just feel so depressed." Do you know what she said back? She just said, "Oh that's alright, you're at art college, that's what you're meant to do," and we laughed and that was it.

Some parents will still do that but when you're paying thousands of pounds a year in fees, housing costs and everything else, the chances are the that the mother's going to say, "Right, I want to speak to the tutor, I want to see what you've been learning!"

And so I think it's all to do with that and nothing to do with whether it is called a polytechnic or a Bauhaus to be frank.

You had grants as well didn't you?

Yes. Grants, housing benefits and I could also claim the dole when I went home in the summer. There were lots of things I could do like that and that gave me an economic freedom that's now been lost.

There are many students who still do live away from home whilst studying, living on a student loan...

I salute students for their struggles. Though the demonstrations I went on in the late 1980s to stop the loans and keep the grants obviously did nothing. The government carried on anyway.

Why did they take the grants away?

Well it's money isn't it? I remember sometime in Spring 1990 Sussex NUS organised a lobby of an old-style, corpulent Tory MP in Brighton called Julian Amery. At the end of the surgery he took a delegation of students who were protesting against the cuts. One of the older students said to him something to the effect of, "You're creating a situation where only the wealthy elite will be able to go through higher education." He then said something to the effect of, "Well yes of course," and we said, "But that disadvantages working class children." He then said something to the effect of, "Well yes but that depends on whether or not you think that everyone is equal!"

That's not an exact quote but the point is that he expressed a belief in the virtue of elites; that elites were good for the country and that it's better that someone from Eton has an education than some kid from a mill town up North. He didn't necessarily want people like me, from my background, in higher education and he certainly didn't see any virtue in higher education for all. He wanted only people from the elite, the ruling class and those who had the money to afford it to be educated and he was totally unapologetic about that. He clearly saw spending power as a form of 'natural selection'.

No one would be allowed to spout that now. But basically the same thing applies and that's why we have cabinets composed of Etonians, or whatever.

So you're not going to be voting Conservative in the upcoming election then?

[This interview took place just before the May 6th 2010 election that elected out Labour and elected in a Conservative and Liberal democrat coalition government]

(Both laugh)

You can infer what you like! Obviously that's the rationale behind the changes in education and those were the backbenchers that supported Margaret Thatcher's policy. They didn't agree with the principle of 'education for all'.

When I went back to education to train as a teacher I had to take a loan out then.

Do you think all art is assessable and do you think the degree show can fairly accommodate all types of practice – like for example, site-specific or performance work? How do you draw up assessment criteria?
I think art *learning* can be assessed and that doesn't matter or have any fundamental bearing on what the final form of the art is. This is understandably one of the things students are often more vexed about than staff. Staff are artists themselves and see a wide range of work all of the time, but we are also teachers and have a clear set of criteria against which we assess the learning process and the development of each artist. If a student came up to me with a scrunched up piece of paper and said, "That's art," I wouldn't be worried about whether I could assess it or not. I'd be worried about whether they were aware of Martin Creed's work or not – and that

there would form one of the points of discussion amongst staff in the assessment meeting.

The point is that there are precedents for all sorts of things. It's not hard to assess amazing work. The assessment criteria we use are nationally agreed benchmarks.

Oh are they, for all of the universities?
Yes, of course. That's why we have external examiners. HEFCE (Higher Education Funding Council for England) draw up broad benchmarks and parity between universities is something that we pay very close heed to. To demonstrate, someone from Goldsmiths is currently on the board of external examiners for this course.

So both universities have the same assessment criteria?
In terms of the national benchmarks, yes. HEFCE monitor parity. The individual course might have different emphases, structure or specific course content but none of that is a problem. I was an external examiner for a few years at Wimbledon College of Art for example, which has a different structure. I had to go to their boards, see all the work and I had to question and interrogate any disparity in marking.

There are restrictions though. You can't have two people reciprocating, so I can't go to Goldsmiths at the same time as someone from Goldsmiths is here. People travel up and down the country to ensure that people up and down the country in the same bands have parity of standards.

So I presume that when you see work for the first time you must be presented with it in its context, with supporting work?
Yes. We all mark separately and then all tutors come together to discuss marks. It's amazing how all tutors usually come within one or two given grades of each other. It's very rare that you get very different grades but if

we do we all troop out and look at the work again. That happens across the country. We show these marks to the examiners and if they're happy they're happy but if they're not they say, "Well, I think you should move that band and your 2:2s should be further down," – or further up, or whatever.

Students sometimes forget that assessments are going on all of the time too, by that I mean we make notes on tutorials and things.

But without a knowledge of its context you couldn't just walk up to a work and announce, "That work's good," could you? Does anyone have the codes to do that?
Well yes and no. It's back to that thing of how art education is different from art practice. I personally might love a piece of work that you do but I have to work out whether my love of that work is accidental. What you're testing when you're looking at the work of a student is whether that standard is consistent. I was reading a review once by Sarah Kent where she said she saw this work and it looked great but then she saw more work in the same show by the same artist and came to think that the good work might have just been a lucky accident.

"Does the artist really understand what they are doing?" That's the point that's interrogated. If someone crunches up the paper and doesn't know what they're doing they're not going to get a good mark. But if someone crunches up Martin Creed's paper and makes a comment on or extends what that work's trying to do and develops that style of practice further, then they will. It's not an arbitrary thing.

How do you think students choose their universities? Are they influenced by brands? And do the universities make the students or do the students make the universities?
It's important to have a good reputation of course. But I didn't go to a 'brand university'. Artists *are* identified by their milieu but how that forms might not necessarily be via an institution. I don't really believe that insti-

tutional brands are the be-all and end-all, though lots of galleries trade on a name, certainly. What I think *is* important is that you develop the skills in someone to make interesting work and that they can take that wherever they are. I'd have hated to be stuck with a brand 'style' in my work.

Do you think there are 'house styles'?
Although institutions have largely dispensed with it, you do sometimes find individual tutors here and there who still fancy that they can promote a personal school style of teaching like there used to be. Where it occurs it's indicative of weak teaching. I think it's important that everyone who teaches art is an artist but not, "Everyone copy me," like the old master style. To a large extent that is dying out generationally. There have been cases of artists who have been marketed under the basis that they studied under Richter or whoever, so if you did, your blurry paintings would have more currency than other blurry paintings. That way of thinking doesn't interest me and I don't think it interests the students who come here. All of the students here are sparky, they always have something to say and I love that. I don't want a brand where no one says anything or everyone's 'too cool for school', because a lot of that is a mask for absolute terror. As long as you facilitate the students to produce interesting work in a humane environment that's what matters.

DERECK HARRIS

Dereck Harris is acting course director for the BA Fine Art courses at Wimbledon College of Art, part of University of the Arts London. We met at the British Museum in May 2010.

What is your position at Wimbledon?
I'm acting course director at the moment, to see if I like it and to see if the institution likes it.

I was running the painting pathway for five years before I did this. The painting pathway is the biggest of the pathways under the fine art umbrella. We have about 180 students whereas the other pathways have about 70. Across the three fine art pathways at Wimbledon there are about 360 students, both full and part-time.

All in all, how long have you been teaching at the college?
I came to Wimbledon about ten years ago and I started as the Drawing Fellow. I then got more and more involved in teaching here after the fellowship finished in 2002.

What did you do before you taught at Wimbledon?
I taught regularly on the part-time BA Fine Art course at Chelsea and at Maidenhead on the Foundation course. I also taught for extended periods at Canterbury and Loughborough, and if you include one-off visits I've taught in a lot of places, gradually building up that side of things whilst still making and showing art.

Did you study art yourself?
Yes. I did my BA at Cardiff from 1980-1983 and then MA Painting at Chelsea from 1985-1986.

Are you trained as a teacher?
No. I'm an artist who got into teaching, the same as many people from my generation and the generation before. Now the whole sector is changing and it's becoming increasingly professionalised. A lot of colleges looking to fill posts will be looking for those who have a Post Graduate Certificate for Learning and Teaching qualification and in the future they will be looking for a PhD qualification too.

For those who've not had experience?
Yes. I think if you have a substantial amount of experience then to a certain extent you're insulated from those requirements. I've lived through a transition phase. PhDs barely existed when I began whereas now they've become much more established. Research culture means that fine art has now incorporated PhD supervision of original research in the way that other established academic disciplines have traditionally done.

What made you decide to teach?
I enjoyed it and it was also a financial imperative as I needed to earn a living. I'd done a number of other things for a number of years but I'd found them less rewarding and intellectually un-engaging.

Part of the enjoyment of teaching comes from the sense of satisfaction gained from the belief that you're helping other people on their journey of self-development by passing on your own knowledge and experience.

Is that the bit that's important? Can you actually teach art or is it more about this 'passing on of experience'?

That's the sixty million dollar question really isn't it? I don't think you can teach genius and I don't know if you can teach pure originality or iconoclastic verve. What you can do is put the conditions into place whereby students can experience a level of intense debate and experience self-reflection. Students get to know themselves and learn about their own personalities, strengths and weaknesses. Staff can also help students determine what their own interests are.

Because there is a certain amount of self-realisation involved in the fine art education experience, it is slightly different I think, to the applied arts, such as graphic design or fashion. Fine art is also very different to a lot of other established academic disciplines in the humanities because of its emphasis on creativity over canonical knowledge and historical analysis. Perhaps creative writing is more closely related to fine art?

If you teach for a while you become better at communicating and more sensitive to the psychological character of the student with whom you are conversing. In terms of things like building confidence or the use of criticism to challenge, you become better at judging situations and adapting your approach for each individual student. You also develop a competence for group teaching situations and learn how to lead collaborative discussion and maintain the intensity of intellectual exchange.

These are all skills that you could describe as pedagogic or teaching skills, whereby you help people out. People can learn themselves over a period of time – and that is known as auto-didactic learning – but it is invariably slower and takes longer.

Does pedagogy differ between institutions?

Inevitably there are differences yes. Over the last 20 years, within the context of the transition to professionalisation, art schools have changed. They have gone from being very individual, where the student experience of a particular school was flavoured by the individual personalities of the staff, to the opposite – a system. The latter idea of how best to teach art, is to set assignments, encourage problem solving, and integrate groups of students. This current learning and teaching culture optimises different types of teaching strategies like one-to-one tutorials, group tutorials, seminars, lectures and breakout discussion groups after lectures to aid the digestion of the content.

What was the Bologna Treaty?
The Bologna Treaty is having a greater impact in Europe but it is essentially an attempt to export the Anglo-American BA and MA modularised higher education system to all European higher education colleges.

Are there still differences between institutions or has art education become standardised?
There are still differences but they are more subtle. The influence of Goldsmiths College is pervasive and one of its legacies is the broad-based fine art course. Those who have gone through the Goldsmiths experience refer to the aggressive character of the convener group critique, a method used to break down the values and assumptions of a student. This process seems to be not simply about questioning, but instead challenging to the point of dismantling certain assumptions, perceptions, propositions or beliefs that incoming students have. The responsibility then remains to rebuild or reconstruct the student's artistic identity – and perhaps this is the overall aim of the course?

So that's a pedagogical model. It's not one that I agree with but I can see that some Goldsmiths alumni have made very interesting art and some have been very successful. There is no doubt something to be said for it, for the right kind of conforming student. However, in my view this approach can lead to a conceptual, stylistic or attitudinal homogeneity.

What model does Wimbledon use?

Wimbledon is probably more democratic and we advocate a diversity of attitudes and approaches in our methods for supporting students as they go through the course. We have widening participation (WP) initiatives in place that have been implemented by the New Labour government and so we encourage students from 'non-traditional' backgrounds to study here. By this I mean so-called 'first generation' students who are the first in their family to go to university as well as students from Black or Minority Ethnic (BME) backgrounds. We also encourage diversity in terms of the type of subject matter that students might address, the kind of stylistic tropes they might adopt, and the types of making technologies and techniques that might evolve. We aim to catalyse joined up thinking between these elements of practice, believing that a synthesis of these components can form an artistic identity.

Building genuine and sustainable self-confidence, challenging beliefs, and fostering a place for authentic creative engagement with an educational experience is complicated. Learning and self-development require the right equilibrium of laboratory conditions, and recent pedagogic research has shown that social integration catalyses an open-ended and enquiring learning environment.

If you have a more open, pluralistic approach, without an institutional agenda or an over-instrumentalised pedagogic structure, you're more likely to foster confidence in students across a broader range of attitudes and approaches, resulting in a diversity of voices as fine art practice.

So Wimbledon's approach lends itself to being more broadly supportive?

Well it's more supportive than the caricature I drew of the Goldsmiths convener-group culture! It's also a smaller institution, with a small campus at arms length from the centre of London. The smallness engenders a friendly atmosphere and students really engage with this and frequently comment upon it. Although friendliness is a key factor, it goes hand-in-hand with subject-specific learning and critical rigour. I do not think these two are mutually exclusive and I would argue that they are symbiotic.

You mentioned subject-specific learning …
Wimbledon offers subject-specific fine art provision. In contrast, I think it is possible to generalise that a large majority of the fine art courses in the UK conform to the broad-based fine art model. I would say that most of these courses privilege teaching methods that conform to an orthodoxy of 'prior-conceptualisation' in their approach to art making. What I mean by this is that the discussion of ideas often precedes – and can inhibit – the making process itself.

Can you expand on why this might be?
The currency of conceptualism in the contemporary art world is very powerful and for good reason. The last thirty years of art practice has illuminated the artist's intention and so the pressure to devise a conceptual platform for a student's developing art practice is significant.
But the aesthetic component of art making requires skill-base, a work ethic, studio discipline, and most importantly the verve of risk taking. Wimbledon advocates a process of 'thinking through making' – successive cycles of production and reflection, rather than the orthodoxy making after thinking: 'prior-conceptualisation'.
Do you remember the model I was describing at the beginning of this transition period, of the small colleges individually led by strong personalities?

Yes.

Those colleges often promoted a very particular agenda, which might have reflected the opinions or prejudices of a small group of staff. I think that way of teaching is analogous to the atelier system.

What does atelier mean?
It's the French word for studio. The atelier system is still established in German art schools.

What does it involve?
One highly visible practising artist, often a painter, runs the course in their studio and their own practice, beliefs and experience dominate the discourse in which students are immersed. Students have to find a relationship with that context and they either agree with it or they push away from it and find the confidence to stand outside. The system is rooted historically in the studio tradition of an old master painter like Rubens or Titian, where craft and skills-base were taught to the apprentice under the auspices of the 'artisan'.

What was your own art education like?
My education from 1980-1984 encompassed the change we have been talking about. When I started, the staff were pretty much an exclusively male team, made up of mid-to-late career painters, who in their formative years had been heavily influenced by the American vanguard of Abstract Expressionism – which was happening over in America and then the UK in the sixties. The small size of the team and the agenda set by them was I think, typical of a lot of what was happening across the country. I can say that as a result of discussions with people I've come to know since.

When I started teaching in 1993 on a foundation course, there was a similar ethos in place. But since then I have been part of implementing some of the changes that have been commented on in the Art Monthly articles.

What initiated these changes?
Around the early sixties, the government decided to commit to mandatory public funding of student grants for all students accepted onto a BA.

The art and design sector were offered BA status, together with the promise of funding, but would need to develop a traditionally accepted 'academic component' of the course. That is to say that strings were attached. That was a major development and it meant that part of the curriculum needed to take the form of theoretical – now called 'contextual' – written work. The requirement for a written dissertation was necessary in order to qualify for the final award. That was the beginning of academicising fine art as a subject area.

Incidentally there are now a higher percentage of fine art courses per capita in the UK than anywhere else in the world; certainly more than in Europe and North America where there are very established contemporary art markets, particularly in Germany and the US.

But the British public's attitude towards contemporary art remains at best one of tolerance and at worst, one of deep suspicion that it is fundamentally deceitful and bogus. This is an unfortunate misunderstanding and is in part a reflection of the innate anti-intellectualism prevalent in the UK.

The UK is unlike France or Germany for example, where the History of Ideas, as well as the basic tools of philosophical thought, religious faith and ideological thinking, are taught as part of the National Curriculum. The British state school curriculum does not engage with the history of ideas and goes no further than religious education when covering belief systems, ethics and comparative moral values.

So do you think then that the British public's suspicion and misunderstanding of contemporary art is a failing of our state school system to cover it and tools for thinking through ideas in the curriculum?
Yes. I think that the state school system does let contemporary art down and it does not prepare citizens to engage with a dialogue about ideas and values; for example, the ability to start a dinner party discussion about why we value the things we value. Contemporary art can function as a conversation piece in the context of a hosted social environment, where

the owners exhibit their collection as a series of signs and signifiers of their intellectual and emotional values.

Do you think that art education is better now or do you think something has been lost?
Most people say we have lost something and I agree that some things have been compromised and others constantly diminished. However, some things have improved.

Can you give examples?
OK. Let's think about the kind of dedication that some artists brought to the act of teaching, the way they considered it their 'calling'. The decision to become an artist in the first place was because they saw themselves as some sort of cultural worker, and saw participating in discussions about art, disseminating ideas and engaging with students, as part of that. For these people, artistic and intellectual activity forms it's own kind of capital outside of the idea of a 'creative industries career' and outside of the mainstream idea of financial capital.

So there was more of the above going on in the unprofessionalised era and the interplay between staff and students relaxed, testing the boundaries of authority. That system allowed for more autonomy and it was less regulated. In its best manifestations you had some really good colleges with staff really inspiring students and a remit to establish a course with the emphasis on risk-taking and not too much concern for outcomes, prescribed learning objectives, or accreditation at assessment points.

I still say to students who are new to Wimbledon that the most important part of their experience is the ongoing journey and the continuum of their practice. The assessment points act as milestones; points of reflection along the way, and when they leave the course it's not the end of something, just a kind of checking point on their progress.

I am sceptical about the PG Cert and some of the other so called 'instrumentalised' aspects of learning and teaching where I believe these values are not supported. I have reservations about the continued advance of the sector into academic professionalisation. More and more people are coming in to teach on fine art courses and aren't necessarily practising artists. They may be researchers, theorists or academics and they are increasingly unlikely to have that sense of vocational commitment – no interest in a commitment beyond the call, so to speak. Such a member of staff would arrive at work on time and leave on time.

I think the better colleges are those committed to what I'm framing as a more 'authentic' art school ethos and are staffed by practising artists.

At the beginning of this interview you made the distinction between a fine art practitioner and a researcher. Can you expand on this?
The definition of research in fine art is inherited from the sciences via the humanities. It requires the researcher to identify a research question and to establish their research methodology, whereby, for example data may be statistically interpreted. That method of research works very well, *in the sciences*. It works less well in some of the humanities and I don't think it fits with art at all and I think a lot of artists feel the same way. The Arts and Humanities Research Council (AHRC) is the government's instrument for administering research funds across these academic subject areas. The AHRC has so far been unable or unwilling to investigate other definitions of research for the Art and Design sector.

Of course there are lots of people who will grasp the opportunity to frame what they do with a research question and an appropriate methodology, so there is no shortage of people prepared to sign up as fine art researchers. But they are not necessarily doing what artists do or what the organic peer-review mechanism of the 'art world' recognises as art. And therein lies the tension.

We may be looking at a whole different community of staff for the future art school. To a certain extent this is what has happened in America where the Fine Art PhD culture has been established for longer.

What do you think of practical craft-based skills, should they be taught?
That's another speech coming up now! I think it depends. We'll start with the idea of what art is. Is art actually an ideas based activity or is it about an aesthetic encounter? I think really it's both.

Certainly for myself and for most of the staff who work in the painting team, we were drawn to make art because we were aesthetically engaged in the making process. For me that's the fundamental starting point. You need technical skills. Craft skills such as drawing and painting are essential skills that need to be taught. Students on courses that don't support these kinds of skills can become very preoccupied with conceptual agendas and may assume that a deskilled art practice signifies sophistication: purposeful incompetence – the slacker aesthetic…or something like that. I think you need to have a generic level of skill in the first place before you can deskill as a conceptual strategy.

Does Wimbledon teach practical skills?
Yes. First year painting students attend a series of workshops that teach them about preparing canvases, traditional methods and also contemporary use of industrial paints and resin. In the case of painting, object-making or object-based sculpture, one does need more extensive practical skills and it takes a good couple of years of making and failing to get to something that's worth looking at. I think a lot of students engaging with new media fine art practice – which includes photography, video, digital media, projection, installation and so on –also need specialised, tailored inductions. Having said this, some of the skills required to engage with new media are fairly generic and most untrained people can pick up a camera and point and click to produce something that can be presented to an audience. In the end it's important to offer the appropriate level of technical instruction for the medium, and beyond that the work will be assessed on a creative level.

This is one reason why we have preserved the subject specific structure of the three pathways within fine art at Wimbledon.

Because you can provide subject-focused skills workshops?
Yes. The pathway system also fosters a peer learning dynamic and a competitive studio work ethic where the development of practical skills are valued.

How many workshops do students attend?
We're talking once or twice a week over a six or seven week period for a couple hours a time. These are offered over and above the standard health and safety inductions to workshops and equipment. At Wimbledon we benefit from an outstanding painting technician, who further supports student development on an individual basis. It's not a huge amount of provision or a very intensive series of workshops but it is an appropriate amount of support during the early part of the course. I think it's invaluable in terms of giving the students a bit of confidence to handle materials – an injection of craft blended into their understanding of fine art.

I think it's equally important to then embed all of that in a very lively contextual studies programme so that students understand themselves, their own thinking and ideas, and then try to understand their work within a broader context.

There are a lot of people I know on certain courses who paint – or rather want to paint, but there's a lack of material guidance.
Self taught.

Yes. And whilst they could proceed this way, something about this lack of material guidance exposes them to criticism geared towards their lack of competence at painting and knowledge of materials. There are technical workshops in London that can help one develop, but with these huge tuition fees shouldn't these be provided for by art schools?
I think that they should yes, no question.

So how far do you think that an absence of such workshops in many colleges is an economical choice and how far is it pedagogical?
Well I think it's both. I've just been reading the article by JJ Charlesworth in Art Monthly. He's talking about the University of the Arts London (UAL) and the amount of money they generate over an annual cycle and the proportion of that money that goes into teaching. He's saying it's less than half but I believe that the norm across the country is less than this.

It's important to understand the particular challenges each institution faces. UAL have a large number of buildings spread across London. Those buildings all need libraries, estates staff, canteens…and these 'central costs' are top-sliced before the funding gets to the course directors and teaching teams. There are real demands on the funds outside of the teaching arena.

There's always a squeeze on resources and if you're running a course you have to prioritise your budgets and you must always support the things that you believe are most important. I think that skills are important in terms of a painting or sculpture courses and that technical induction is very important for fine art media courses too. Other broad-based fine art course directors may not prioritise allocation of resources to practical skills-based workshops. Some course leaders believe that subject matter and content are indexed from theoretical and contextual understanding and as a result they may choose to focus their resources on studio-based seminars in the belief that they are more effectively promoting the discussion of ideas. This approach tends to be more typical and is less expensive to deliver but can result in the over-emphasis of a conceptual rationale that precedes the making of work. It's the prior-conceptualisation process I described earlier.

How much can you tell me about the histories of UK art education?
If I can point to an interesting conference that took place in America – that may help me get to some points about UK art education. The conference was about the future of art education at the art school at Cooper Union for the Advancement of Science and Art in 2009. Thierry de Duve, a French

philosopher who has written extensively on contemporary art, was invited to speak at the conference. He commented on the difficulty of looking at the future of art education without reflecting on its history. Broadly speaking, De Duve proposed that if we trace the history of our European art school inheritance, we can identify some key periods of paradigm shift.

(Takes out a pen and paper and begins to draw a diagram.)

We start with the nineteenth century 'Academy' of connoisseurship, highly honed skills in drawing and painting – directed towards the mimetic depiction of nature, and shared almost exclusively white male community. De Duve summarised this as:

Talent – Metier – Mimesis

The Academy was overthrown by the Salon des Refusés, and the rise of the avant-garde – modernism and the Bauhaus – in the early part of the twentieth century. Subject specificity and primacy of the medium came into play with the Bauhaus model. The teaching strategy followed a democratic idea that every individual's potential could be served by the model of:

Individuality – Medium – Invention

This would propose the idea that anyone could demonstrate his or her creativity through a meritocratic realisation of creative invention or pure artistic potential.

Since then the cross-disciplined teaching of ideas has superseded the base certainty of pure modernist ideology. The conflation of intellectual doubt and philosophical deconstruction have resulted in a post-modern paradigm of pluralism – summarised by de Duve as follows:

Attitude – Practice – Deconstruction

In terms of the present moment broad-based fine art courses have become a norm, and this reflects the permissive attitude of postmodernity. Medium specificity has been broken down in the belief that a pluralism of means equates with interdisciplinary dialogue and conceptual diversity.

I think the easy assumption that the post-modern polymath is best placed to teach the subject is something I just don't agree with. I think at the moment you can create a better fine art learning experience for students by combining the best of De Duve's paradigm models: modernity and postmodernity.

Looking ahead, a further paradigm shift is probably imminent. The most recent discussions around the 'curatorial turn' of ideas about practice, which connect to the context of Relational Aesthetics, have suggested that a future structure might signal a move away from the primacy of artistic individuality and the centred authorship of the self altogether. A speculative model might look like this:

Practice – Collaboration – Reconstruction

That's fascinating, thank you. So does Wimbledon combine a hybrid of models two and three?

Yes. We have subject-specific areas but then we have structures in place to bring the students together in a broader cross-course, cross-year critique. The subject boundaries provide something for students to push against, a process that facilitates independent thought and deepens and particularises their enquiry. I can say this with confidence because of the strength of the graduates coming out of Wimbledon over the last few years and the evidence of their achievements in the professional context.

You could argue that the atelier system provided a similar framework of firm parameters, albeit personality driven. The boundaries force a student to take a position and take responsibility for determining their own identity.

Does an emphasis on the conceptual or a market-influenced search for 'newness' have a detrimental effect on students and their art production?

The search for newness is consistent with the valuing of 'originality' or 'invention' in the second model I drew. I would say that there is no immediate issue with this language but that the problem is more insidious. As the twentieth century wore on, the modernist avant-garde value of originality was sometimes superseded by a new critical imperative of socio-political emancipation. If an artwork was critically received as *transgressive*, then the confirmation of originality was acknowledged and more importantly, a conceptual legitimacy was conferred. The currency of socio-political relevance defined the work's 'edge'.

At the same time the commercial power of the art market has grown, and some sociologists have commented that artworks present similar exchange value to a fine wine, or a rare antique. The contemporary art collector may be as interested in the cultural capital demonstrated by the inventiveness of the work or it's Marxist critique as they are in its novelty and entertainment value. Understandably, young artists striving for originality or transgressive edge in their work can also be influenced or even motivated by a desire to succeed as an internationally collected artist with a highly visible profile. Here lie the seeds of compromise and intellectual dissolution.

This scenario confuses and conflates cultural capital with commercial value and can lead to a situation of art trivialised by the market as artwork that is increasingly collected and exchanged as a novel commodity. The art market will always develop an appetite for novel new commodities to collect. Artists can be pressured to respond to this opportunity, and we turn full circle as some are tempted to present 'transgressive' shock art or relational events with the radical aura of a conceptual art provenance.

Getting back to the shop floor teaching at Wimbledon, in the case of painting, a "What's your concept?" approach to academic tutorial teaching mitigates against sophistication. Straight away the question is pressurising the students to contextualise the work's enquiry and prepare a theoretically robust framework, all in advance of material experimentation. This is an example of the kind of disproportionate pressure that can follow from too much emphasis on prior-conceptualisation.

I would say the way students learn is partly intuitive. In terms of 'intentionality' – a term we use a lot at Wimbledon – we are asking the students to identify their intention and take responsibility for what they're trying to communicate. We encourage them to think about intellectual layering, conceptual strategies, metaphor, critique, poetic space, and to consider the audiences role in the reception of the work. Assessing intentionality in work is complicated and is undertaken by two or more staff that negotiate as a team.

Painters and object makers sometimes negotiate their intentionality through an intuitive or retrospective process. That process though is not valued in the context of some fine art courses where tutorials can prescribe the ordering of ideas and strategies in advance of the making of an object. In these courses conceptual activity is prioritised over all else.

How does education take place, how does the education in a crit or tutorial session actually happen?

Well. Now you're asking! How does learning happen?

In any given teaching scenario the process can be analysed and broken down into constituent parts, though of course during the delivery it doesn't feel like that.

It is important to distinguish between the work, the art, and the pedagogic process. Whilst in the student's experience these are synthesised, in the mind of the lecturer they are somewhat distinct and separate.

The relationship between intention and outcome is a key dynamic that we test, probe and even interrogate in the crits at Wimbledon. It is very valuable for a student to be able adapt to the role of audience for the benefit of the other students in the group. By this I mean that they apply themselves as active members of the audience to try and understand or evaluate the successes of the work of their peers. Of course, in order to do this they need to identify or at least speculate about the intention of their peer's work.

It is also very important for students to develop an understanding of critical or objective distance from their own work. This in turn enables them to evaluate their own attempts to make synthesized artwork and resolve the interrelation between form and content. So they evaluate their choice of means, making technologies, content, subject matter, their awareness of context, understanding of visual languages, conceptual strategies, poetic resonance and so on. All of this integrates in the viewing experience. When the synthesis starts to work well and the reception of the end result is experienced in an integrated aesthetic encounter, then things are starting to really work. Work that sustains thoughtful reflection and an engagement with ideas through the visual senses is close to being art. There – it's easy really.

You were talking earlier about widening participation. Did you yourself grow up seeing art?
No. No one in my family went to university, although my father got a teaching qualification and taught Physical Education in schools for a while.

When was the first time you saw contemporary art?
I saw it in the Sunday papers and my aunt bought me a book on Cezanne when I was fourteen. I knew I was always interested in art as I was good at drawing and painting at school and always found it engaging. I went on to do a foundation course and once you are at college you start seeing a lot more art and talking to people.

I was the same. The first time I saw contemporary art was when I was 18. I find it interesting how you grow up seeing art in a particular way, adopting the same tastes and values as your family, but then you come into a different world where it feels as though you then have to switch your sensibilities and taste over-night.

Well yeah. The widening participation initiative is all about recognising this idea of people coming from non-traditional backgrounds like us and putting extra support in place to help.

There is also a divide between the A-level art experience and HE, which exists because there are very different educational remits going on at A-level and art school. More recently a number of sixth form colleges have started running foundation courses. The Bauhaus foundation idea, which we recognise as 'art school', is now permeating art education in schools.

The main differences stem from the nature of intellectual inquiry and the ingredient of criticism. If you think of art doing a job, operating as a mirror on society and presenting a visual reflection of the way we live, analysis and criticism of society is the core galvanising force that motivates a lot of artists and is a very powerful aspect of cultural work. In order to make art that effectively commentates on injustice or attempts to transgressively shock people out of their complacency, you need to understand your tools and master your means. This involves skills, but also judgement, control and subtlety. A student needs to learn about the synthesis of form and content in their own work and they need to resolve this relationship in order to engage an audience and move or affect them.

Do you think that those who grew up seeing art are at more of an advantage when interpreting art than those who didn't?
Probably yes. If you come from a middle class family that's been based in London or the home counties, if you've been to galleries since you were two years old, if there's lots of books around the house on art and if you go to see plays and music etc, then you have an awful lot of education by the time you arrive at art school. You'd come into a crit – which is about looking at an object, about analysing it and asking questions such as, "How do we decode it?" or, "How do we find it intelligible?" – and if you were of the background I have just described, then you will have a greater knowledge-base to start with than a student who has just moved down from the provinces and has not seen much contemporary art. But I think if you have a

mix of students in a year group then they all learn from each other and test each other and it can almost even out.

What do you think about 'independent learning'?
Self-directed learning is central to the philosophy of running a fine art course. Some of the recent articles published in Art Monthly were saying that in its inception, the model of self-directed learning was radical for the time and a challenge to the atelier system. It challenged the idea that the master knew more than the student and so it challenged his authority. Student centred learning is much more empowering in that politicised sense of neutralised authority in the studio situation.

Some of the published articles were suggesting that the student-centred model has now become the norm, and that the politicised context has subsided as a consequence. They suggest that this can result in staff deferring their teaching duties in favour of admin duties, of which there are many. There are very real systemic audit culture pressures that engineer this situation and place all course leaders in universities under significant pressures. In some institutions the staff may not deliver more than a couple of tutorials per term and let the students get on with it. The point here is that this current situation has evolved without that sense of revolution, opposition or political engagement with an institution and doesn't have the same context.

I am a little ambivalent on this position. I believe that authority can be challenged in a number of small ways all of the time; from the scrutiny of body language – that of the staff – to the empowerment of students to critique the course in direct relation to their experience.

I also think that there are ways of critiquing your employer or host institution by operating within the administrative culture of the host system.

So you mean the current pedagogical system has become more of a tired norm than a politicised educational idea?

This is what commentators are proposing and it's certainly possible that the new member of staff, fresh with their PG Cert may not value or understand the political dynamic of the questioning and shaping of authority that has been handed down to them.

Without a political imperative a lot of commentators would say that fine art has lost its purpose. That's a deeper philosophical question about art education and the way it can be delivered. The suspicion is that this deep professionalization and increasing academicisation of the subject will mean that the historic definition is threatened and lost. In the current situation we are training young people who come with an expectation of a future career in the creative industries. This objective is starting to displace the idea of a moral commitment and vocational drive to make art, agitate within society, or promote dissent and critical discourse. A lot of the artists I know are concerned about this situation.

Do you think that people come to art school now because of a desire for a career? Do art college brands emphasise this?
Yes I think so and I think students do come because of the brand and reputation of a college. Reputation has always been a huge marketing tool used to enhance recruitment and the significance of a college brand becomes all the more important with the introduction and fees. We all know now that the current government is removing public subsidy for university study in the arts and humanities. If applicants are drawn into the idea of being a part of the creative industries that presupposes that there is a career there waiting for them. That's not an unreasonable assumption or expectation but I think that many fine art graduates have elusive career paths. They tend to value cultural capital over mainstream conformity and be resourceful in finding unexpected routes to employment.

Was there less pressure when you were studying?
Yes there was. There was also a smaller art market than there is in the UK

today and nothing like the level of interest and commerce. But even this new expanded art industry centred in London is nothing like the scale that would be required to support the increasing number of graduates emerging each year. There are something like 149 art courses in the UK producing anything from 20 to 60 graduates per year. You start doing the sums over ten years and it's a large community of graduates.

The most committed and ambitious will generally gravitate towards London and will join the community of emerging artists in the East End. As an emerging artist you have a show and if the show has a buzz and your peers are talking about it, that's how an exhibiting career can start. Many others will gravitate towards teaching careers in schools, administration posts and postgraduate education.

Why has there been such an increase in the number of students?
This background of change over the last 20 years has also been informed by the previous Labour government's policy to expand the proportion of the country that is in higher education. Their objective was to put 50 per cent of the population in HE. That objective is essentially emancipatory and serves the principal of avant-garde culture, as it is political change for the better.

Mergers have also come about as a direct result of the New Labour policies. Small art colleges, which I mentioned earlier, are expensive to run, they involve much duplication of facilities such as libraries, estate services and canteens. The small independent art colleges were obliged to merge with universities that have large scale centralised services. They already had the infrastructure and systems for regulating academic quality and so were geared up to accommodate the expansion in student numbers.

Like Wimbledon becoming a part of the University of the Arts London?
Yes, and we have to fight our corner within the University in order to maintain our identity.

We spoke of the increased expectations that students now hold of getting a career. But circumstances have changed. For example, when you were studying, did you receive a full grant?

Yes. We were very fortunate. The system now seems to be moving increasingly towards the American model where fees will grow and grow. Spending cuts will hit higher education hard because many people don't think of it as an essential service. If the cuts keep on escalating it will mean a wholesale revision of the work we do. All the good work New Labour has done in expanding the numbers of those entering higher education will be reversed. The liberal art subjects will always suffer in the context of a recession because society thinks it doesn't need liberal arts graduates to generate wealth. So as we move towards the American model of full fee-paying home students for all arts and humanities subjects, some university courses will struggle to recruit and be forced to close. Universities UK has recognised the jeopardy in this and at the end of last year published a report that put the value of the creative industries at £60 billion to the economy. It made the case for the contribution of humanities and the arts to society. That argument was made against a very particular background.

The so-called STEM subjects – Science, Technology, Engineering and Maths – will continue to receive government subsidy and be tailored to feed industry needs. There will be a stronger form of private subsidy coming into courses; university fees will probably increase *significantly* and all that will dramatically affect the nature of the courses.

This will be very worrying for fine art departments established in the provinces because the art world in this country is centred in London.

You work with Terry Smith. He had an article published in Art Monthly in which he talked about scrapping assessments, the dissertation and scrapping the degree show. Do you agree?

I read that article. I agree with some of the ethos of what Terry says but not the alternative methods he suggests at all. Liam Gillick wrote a letter in Art Monthly too and whilst they perhaps aren't saying the same thing, there is a similarity in what they are proposing in the shared objective of a kind of 'institution without walls' – the idea of an art college without the managerial corporate agenda promoting the 'creative industries' and topping up the top-up fees.

These alternatives *sound* great but I'm afraid they would only ever amount to an elite forum for very engaged and very fortunate young aspiring artists. In terms of any educational revolution that might transform the expectations and opportunities of a significant section of society, I'm afraid it is a non-starter. Your 'widening participation' crowd would simply not engage and not be transformed at all.

The whole point of New Labour's higher education remit was to engage a larger section of society. They have proposed an anti-elitist programme in higher education and people coming from a WP or BME background need a whole lot more structure and a whole lot more support in making that transition from the family environment they've grown up in. So if you don't have all those milestones of assessments and legions of support officers, study skills tutors, counsellors, accommodation advisers and so on, then it will not work. Those vast numbers of students would not get the support they need and simply disengage from the course and go back to work in the local supermarket.

Terry is largely talking about his own experience as someone who came from a non-traditional background and was exceptionally lucky and got very engaged in his course. He studied at Goldsmiths and had a very successful rapport with Michael Craig Martin – but I don't think you can say that the model of his experience works as an educational strategy across society.

What he's saying is, "Let's have a bonfire." Joseph Beuys saw his degree work as training work. I think most artists a year or two after they graduate, would say that they don't feel attached to the body of work they created at art school and that they don't see it as being important now. But it helped them get to where they are now and achieve a level of self-knowledge and self-realisation.

And of course it sounds wonderfully anarchistic saying, "Blast the dissertation, blast the assessment, let's have a bonfire," but it's not practical in terms of helping so many people achieve a form of liberation in their lives, move on from the limiting circumstances of their family background and have a lot more opportunity. And that's a hugely worthwhile thing to be able to achieve.

But a degree show that carries up to 80 per cent of a student's final mark is a very stressful thing to go through though. Is it not too huge a pressure?
It is pressure true, but with the course at Wimbledon all assessments are by exhibition right from the word 'go' and so it's something students are used to and something they understand. The reason we have that in place is because it's the professional model. If one was to aspire to be an artist and have a gallery represent them then that is the name of the game and it's important as a student that you have a go at that.

There may be some art practices now, relational art practices for example, that don't really fit the form of a degree show. But the degree show can migrate and evolve and increasingly it will have to negotiate students doing theirs off-campus in a site-specific context or in a virtual space. All of that is possible.

I think the fundamental message is, "Take responsibility for your decisions, believe in your work and put something out there." Stop saying, "I never finish anything," and, "I want the audience to invent the meaning," – two common mantras amongst current undergrads! That's a huge challenge but it's the completion of a body of work and that's how most artists function, through cycles of initiating, developing, evolving and then presenting a piece of work. Even if artists work collaboratively or across disciplines they always have an end product that can engage and benefit audiences. On some level a constituent part of art is communication and emotional or intellectual engagement. To reject this is not constructive.

In terms of the dissertation, we have these discussions at work endlessly, especially in the context of widening participation or if a student is dyslexic. They may really struggle with written work but we believe they can do it if they really apply themselves. They learn so much from it and it can be a life changing experience. It can certainly have an enormous impact on the focus and strength of the artwork as students go through this academic boot camp.

You said that the degree show should account for off-site and relational work etc. But at the moment it doesn't?
That would be a much more legitimate criticism *if* students working in these areas were genuinely disadvantaged. At Wimbledon we have second year placements, where students go off-campus and do group shows, interventions, public art pieces etc and that can be built upon. If students want to do something off campus for the degree show, there is a structure that could be developed and negotiated. We have had the odd student trying this and of course there are logistical problems like: how do you get your assessors and the external examiners to go to ten different places in London? But these are minor challenges for which there will be solutions.

What would the solutions be?
That's one for me to really take away and think about with my colleagues. You could put more money in it to facilitate teaching time. Or my immediate response is that work ought to be possible to assess through its documentation and some sort of discussion about the intention. It's not ideal but I think a lot of the success of the work can be gauged in that way ... but I am just speculating about a question that I have put to myself.

There are examples where the institution does legally have to accommodate things. For example, if somebody is disabled and can't present or verbally discuss their work in front of their peers for whatever reason, we're obliged to find an alternative form of assessment for those individuals. This is known as accommodated assessment. It follows that if we can do it for those reasons we ought to do it for the reasons you mention. I'm sure that if there was a question on the National Student Survey (NSS) asking, "Do you feel your degree show was marked in the appropriate way?" and the response was negative, the following year would see this become an institutional priority.

In institutions, particularly at the University of the Arts London, there is an enormous amount of anxiety centred on the National Student Survey. The University of the Arts London is positioned at the wrong end of the league and has been for a few years. It would be falsely modest of me not to mention that the Wimbledon BA Fine Art NSS score was amongst the highest across the University.

JOHN AIKEN

....

John Aiken is the professor and director of the Slade School of Fine Art,
part of University College London. It is a post he has held since 2000.
He had already been head of graduate sculpture at the school since 1982.
We met in his office in May 2010.

....

How long have you been teaching on this course for?
I was appointed as head of graduate sculpture in 1982. Then I became Slade
professor and director in 2000. So I've been teaching here for 28 years.

Wow. And before that?
Before that I also taught at a number of different art schools as a part-time
and full-time member of staff. I taught in Belfast, Newport and sometimes
abroad. I studied at Chelsea School of Art.

*A lot of tutors are artists and have never trained as teachers. Now though it is
widely preferred by institutions that tutors have a teaching qualification. What
is your opinion on this?*
I don't have a formal teaching qualification! Personally I don't think tutors
need one. I think there's a danger going on in art schools now whereby
the more we have to engage in formal academic procedures such as the
Research Exercise, the more the academic disciplines of other subject areas
such as the sciences are impacting on how art is taught. I think there has
been an over-academicisation of our subject, the subject of fine art. As a
result of that I think a lot of people who see themselves as practising artists
have been, to a certain extent, disenfranchised from working in art education because they don't want to be involved in the processes, procedures
and mechanisms of how art is taught in art school now.

How does this differ from when you were at art school?
When I started at art school it was very much done the opposite way. The focus was on how to get leading contemporary artists into art schools to give tutorials. They didn't have to fill in forms, they didn't have to do PhD supervision and they didn't have to do any of those things an academic in an art school now is now required to do. I think you've got a lot of people out in the art world now who associate themselves as artists and academics and a lot of people who associate themselves as artists and don't want to be called an academic. So there's a kind of tension there but I also think that's always existed.

In late sixties and early seventies art school tutoring was seen as a mechanism for supporting artists. One or two days a week of teaching gave you a basis for living and if you sold work beyond that, that was good. But the market was not as sophisticated in the sixties and seventies as it was in the eighties and nineties and as it is in recent days. As the market took off a lot of artists who might have gone into teaching in art schools didn't. So there's a missing generation there. A lot of those who went into art school teaching as artists are now retiring or are now approaching retirement.

There's now another generation that have been part of the academicisation of art and are therefore much more OK with how things work and with grant applications and so on. Certain approaches to making art don't lend themselves well to fitting in with a research context. It's a complex and, I think, often tense relationship between the academic world and the art world.

When did the switch happen and why?
I think the switch started to happen as early as the mid-seventies and it got much more formalised as the art schools became part of polytechnics and then part of universities. Universities are big organisations with a very small art school within them and therefore over time the art schools have had to conform to the universities' rules and mechanisms, which are often

formulated in terms of research around the sciences. The system is not based on the needs of the subject of fine art, that's a minority activity.

To give an example, the Slade makes up 270 students in a university of 20,000. It's quite hard to make your voice heard within a huge institution that's largely built around biomedicine. But on the other hand University College London (UCL) is very supportive of the Slade and wants us to be here. I think a lot of other universities have had a problem assimilating an art school into them because they haven't been used to the space requirements of an art school. They also haven't been used to the one-to-one tutorial regimes that take place in art schools. It's a way of delivering work, which is very alien to both the sciences and the humanities.

So why then did art schools become part of universities?
Funding. Art schools couldn't sustain themselves as small independent institutions so in order to survive they had to go into bigger institutions with centralised finance etc. It has caused a lot of problems but I don't think it's all negative. I think there have been many positive aspects in the development of art schools and as long as they can maintain credibility and the focus on the subject it's OK. It's about how we maintain fine art as a distinct subject but also use the expertise that exists within the bigger institution.

Is there a difference, do you think, in the reasons why students went to art school twenty years ago and why they come now?
It's remarkably the same oddly enough. If you think back 20 years ago to the portfolios you got from applicants and what applicants said in their interviews, some of the names would have changed of the artists they're interested in, though rather remarkably some haven't.

So I don't think it is that different. I think possibly the quality and the number of applicants has gone up. This year we're completely inundated with applications to the point of almost not being able to cope. We had nearly 1400 applicants for the undergraduate course and there are just 35 places, so that works out as one place for every 39 applicants. Within the University that's nearly double our closest department, which is Economics with a ratio of 1:20. So having to look at 1400 portfolios is something that doesn't happen in the rest of the University. On top of that we have 450 postgraduate applications and so the mechanism of selecting the students becomes a major part of the institutions activities and a crucial part of the year as well. It's very nice on one hand but very taxing institutionally on the other.

I think the postgraduate application now is considerably different to what it was in the past because most post-grads have actually spent some or even a long time between finishing their undergraduate degree and applying for their postgraduate degree. We are also getting a large number of exceptionally good applications coming in from all over the world – verging on the point where the overseas applicants have been better than the British applicants.

Why do you think that is?
I think it's because overseas applicants go through a number of cultural changes, often from a highly academic, structured course to one that is embracing contemporary art. They're almost having both aspects, which gives them strength. Some have also had careers before applying to study at postgraduate level and so the debate at this level is quite sophisticated because a lot of experience comes into it.

Why are so many people applying?
I don't know. It could be the recession, because they want to come here, all sorts. Over two years our undergraduate application numbers have doubled. It could also be explained because the mechanism for applications has changed, there used to be two routes and now there's only one.

Can you tell me a bit about your course philosophy?
I would say it is a student-centred philosophy. We want to attract and engage the best possible students in a debate with each other, with staff and with the wider community of UCL. I think our philosophy is very focussed on what the students themselves are doing rather than saying, "This is a philosophy, idea or critical theory that you have to subscribe to." I'd say that the latter is didactic and very much a definition of what we *wouldn't* be doing.

So we're not asking students to subscribe to something, it's more, "We've invited you in, we want to engage with you, develop your ideas within this context and we want to learn something as well." That's the way it should be in my view. We're asking students to develop something within a critical and supportive context, and how that context is nuanced will depend on the body of students at any one time. Art school is a unique environment and once you leave, the environment you enter into might be less critical or it could be more damagingly critical.

Do you think students thrive under and understand this philosophy?
I think students will approach any situation from a variety of perspectives.

Twenty years ago it was a time of grants, which gave students the space and money to carry on with their work. I think it's kind of the opposite now. Some places don't provide any space, or provide meaningless space, and they don't provide any money.

It was very casual in the past. Students came in, there weren't that many seminars, not that many formal opportunities to debate issues and it was more, "I'm an artist, you're an artist, let's have a chat about your work." It wasn't a particularly critically aware context. I think that there was an important change in the eighties and it's been very active ever since then.

Saying that, I think what is missing in a lot of institutions now is a community of lecturers that are all in at the same time. In a lot of institutions the lecturers never meet each other any more because one's in on one day and there will be another one in on another day – and so I think it's really important that the art schools provide a forum for staff to have discussions with each other to catch up. There are very few forums for artists to meet and I think that art schools in the past were what provided that. I think at Slade we still do provide it as on any one day there are ten or so members of staff in and they will discuss things together outside of the framework of delivering the courses. I think that's very positive. We're also in the context of a university where we can discuss things with other members of staff from different faculties over lunch. I think a lot of that is missing in the art school at the moment. There's a forum for the students but not for the staff.

Do you think students are influenced by staff or the rapport between them?
I think they are interested in and influenced by that yes but I wouldn't categorise what students do here as a 'house style'. There are individual voices and those individuals may well collaborate on things but there isn't any notion of, "If you come to the Slade you have to do it this way." Thank God! I mean there might have been at some point but there isn't now.

I think it's really important that you see a huge variety of work that is constantly shifting and constantly developing. You walk around the studios once a week and it's remarkable how different they are from one week to the next. I like to be surprised at the degree show too when I suddenly think, "Oh, my recollection is they were working like this and now they're working like that." So I expect things to be developing all of the time. I don't expect things to just be refined or commodified or developed for the market, even though I know you have to be very conscious of what you're doing afterwards.

Do you think students think about that?
There's a big financial investment being made by students now and I think students are much more aware of, "I've spent all this money on a course, how am I going to retrieve it in what I do?" whereas in my generation that simply wasn't an issue. We were delighted to attend art school.

You had grants?
Yes and no expectation of making money through the market when we left. It was very much a culture of grants. You left art school, you applied for an Arts Council or British Council grant to do an exhibition somewhere, you got a studio and you did some part-time teaching. You might get some funding to do a project but the expectation of selling work was fairly remote.

So do you think students come in with an expectation of having a career in the art market now?
I think they do but they're also pragmatic and realistic about it, which they have to be because we can't rely on it. Saying that, things have opened up in an explosive way and it's hard to count how many galleries there are in London now, or even how many residencies. There are a lot more opportunities out there and a lot of opportunities that artists create for themselves. So it's much more complex.

You mentioned earlier that there is no 'house style' at Slade. I thought that statement was interesting because there has always been this perception amongst students elsewhere that Slade is the more 'materials-led' school, especially when compared to somewhere like Goldsmiths which is perceived to be the 'conceptual' school. This is obviously a stereotype but do you think that it holds any truth? And are you aware of it?
I don't understand that. I think what our students do here is approach work from a whole variety of different perspectives as I'd expect them to do. I also think that 'skill' is a misused word. I think you have to be skilful at whatever you do. If skill is interpreted as craft then that's complete nonsense as far as I'm concerned. It's also complete nonsense to describe the school in that way too.

For example, Angela de la Cruz has just been nominated for the Turner Prize 2010. She was here at the same time as Tomoko Takahashi. Out of a group of six students in sculpture these two have been nominated and not on the basis of their 'traditional skills'. Of other artists that studied at the Slade and received nominations: Martin Creed is somebody who cannot be described as working from a traditional craft-based skill, but actually Martin was incredibly good at that. Rachel Whiteread used skill but wasn't a craft person in terms of traditional skills. Tacita Dean is an extremely good filmmaker but that would not have been deemed to be a traditional skill based activity, and Douglas Gordon's work would be in the same category.

All of these artists have been operating at the cutting edge of contemporary art and have been very skilful in a variety of ways and that's what I would promote. Whatever you're doing you have to be skilful at it. That could be negotiating the art world or learning how to make a piece of work that conveys what you want it to, to best effect. Therefore, to be skill-less would be an inappropriate way of describing Goldsmiths or us. Both institutions promote skill in a very dynamic way.

I guess then, to re-phrase, there is a perception that there is strong support here for people who want to pursue a making or materials-based practice?
Sure. I mean material culture is an extremely important part of contemporary practice and an understanding of materiality and of how you actually do things is extremely important both conceptually and in terms of practice. Angela de la Cruz is a very good example. She was working in the sculpture department and made paintings that she then turned into 3D objects by smashing them. I think she's a good example of an exercise of skilling and de-skilling simultaneously. I think that debate is very active here.

But then you can only 'de-skill' once you have the skill?
Exactly. What I think has been interesting about some overseas students who have come to the Slade for postgraduate study is that they've been

trained in very traditional ways but then they can undermine that through their practice. I think that's why a lot of them come to Britain so that they can develop their work within a contemporary context.

Undergraduate study in the Far East is often very traditional. They go through a whole series of traditional skill-based work activities and a lot of the students who apply from overseas to come here have already done postgraduate courses overseas as well as in Korea or Japan. That just means they've had this very traditional skill-base, then done a Masters course which has taken that into a different level and then they come here. So they come here further ahead than our students who have only done a three year undergraduate degree, often at an institution which has not got or maintained certain processes or is not equipped to deal with fine art in its broader sense. Because we only do fine art, all of our equipment is for fine art. We don't have to share computers with graphic design. Our facilities, whether electronic media or print are exclusively for the use of our students. We also have good relations with architecture, engineering and medicine.

So within a studio context, how we support a studio technically is realistic with how an artist might pursue their career. We can draw on a hugely sophisticated knowledge and hugely sophisticated technical skills within the context of the University to enable students to say, "OK, I can develop my work in that way, I know what it needs to do it and I know what I need to do to support it." I think developing skills in a wide variety of ways, including the ability to be able to talk about your work in a conceptual framework is really important. If an institution isn't covering all this then I think it's failing.

Do you think there are some that don't manage to cover all of that?
The trouble is most institutions can't cover all that and so they promote one thing over another. They do that not because they think it's the best thing to do but because they don't have the support at the level that's necessary. So for example, some institutions got rid of the traditional skills

of printmaking because it was under-subscribed and students didn't want to use it. It was expensive and it took up space and required dedicated technical support.

One of the things we've discovered is that increasingly students embracing digital technologies are returning to analogue technologies and using those both together. If you don't have analogue technologies anymore you can't do that. For me this is a really important part of student development at the moment, this re-discovery of older technologies and a recontextualisation of them within a new framework. It's quite remarkable actually and it almost requires a generation to pass through before that can be addressed properly. My generation was all about deskilling because it was a very vocational set up in art schools in the fifties and early sixties and there was a big wholesale rejection of techniques in the mid to late 1960s when art schools were redefined after the Coldstream Report. Now I think students are questioning what that was all about and thinking instead, "This method looks interesting, I'm going to use it." I think it's a very open way of appropriating, but you need to be introduced to what's 'appropriatable' in order to do that.

Dr MO THROP

....

Dr Mo Throp is the BA Fine Art course director at Chelsea College of Art and Design, part of University of the Arts, London. It is a position she has held for the last six years. We met in her office in May 2010.

....

What did you do before coming to teach at Chelsea?
Most of my previous teaching was done on the MA Fine Art at Goldsmiths. I was also course director of the part-time BA Practice & Theory of Visual Art course at Chelsea for several years. I have also taught PhD students and undergraduate students.

Did you study art yourself?
Yes. I did sculpture at Saint Martins when it was just Saint Martins and have continued to make work since then. That was a pretty traumatic experience!

Why do you say that?
Well without going into the history of that period, which is much talked about now, that course in the late sixties was known as the 'Hot House', dominated by Caro. We were directed to continue that tradition – it was a pretty repressive regime.

Was that the 'Locked Room' phase?
No it was before then, before Peter Kardia took over. I went on to get a DAAD postgraduate scholarship to Berlin, which was fantastically liberating. I then did an MA in Art Theory and also a PhD here at Chelsea. I didn't do these one after another, but spread over several years.

What made you decide to teach?
I was going to say I didn't have that intention but that's not true because after my BA I also did an Art Teachers Certificate (ATC) at Goldsmiths. I enjoy teaching and I probably always wanted to. It came easily.

You have a teaching certificate but many others in your generation don't.
A requirement for HE level art tutors to have such a qualification is becoming increasingly common. But there seems to be a lot of disgruntlement amongst staff towards this idea. What are your views?
Well yes, it is now a requirement that teaching staff have one – but so is having a Ph-bloody-D! It's extraordinary! I think that the 'disgruntlement' was from staff who had been already teaching for several years; nevertheless I have heard that staff who did complete the course while teaching found it positive. In fact the UAL has conceded that staff with a certain amount of experience do not have to complete the PG Cert.

As a course director I get very many enquiries about teaching possibilities. For fine artists teaching is both a livelihood and a community. Increasingly art institutions are focussing on research; although a lot of artists teaching on my course exhibit regularly and are represented by dealers, the college also seeks to involve staff in a community of researchers – within the institution – which can be very positive. It's not like it used to be when I was a student. Thank God!

Why do you say that?
Art education is no longer all in the hands of a particular group of practitioners and friends from the same background; that was certainly my experience of Saint Martins. It was an exclusive club with a few key dealers and galleries.

But the real issue I think you're getting at, is that in those days teaching was your livelihood and your role as an artist was out in the gallery system and those roles had little relation to each other.

That relationship is now slowly beginning to turn around. In the last five years there has been a shift to a research culture in the art school, though that also raises other problems.

Can you explain a bit about what this much heard term 'research culture' means?
Universities, and art schools as part of them, now ask for the research details of their academic staff, even if a tutor only teaches a few hours a year. We fill in a research return and give that information, whatever it is – the more significant and more international it is the better – to the university. Research outputs are graded by the university and this determines the level of funding available from the government.

Previously teaching staff could make bids to their Colleges to support their research. Most staff have research contracts, which gives 20 per cent of our time to research throughout the year. Research status basically gives staff the time to do their own work and to contribute to the institution's research return. That's how universities receive money from the government.

That's fascinating and clarifies a lot, thank you.
I'm trying to tell you all of this though from the point of view of someone who is an artist *and* a teacher, like my staff. They don't want a role like mine. It's pretty difficult to teach – which is quite emotionally exhausting as well – and still stay focussed on continuing to develop your own practice. When posts go from part-time to full-time that becomes a real difficulty and many tutors who this happens to feel that they can no longer be an artist and that the institution 'owns' them. Lots of staff here won't do more than a half time job because they have their career as an artist to think of – even if it might be going badly and they have no income and no shows, they won't give up the rest of their time! Those who do manage to juggle it need to be super organised and focussed.

So the terrible ongoing dilemma is that you have to keep on teaching as there's no other source of money, yet if you do too much that's the end of your career as an artist! There are opportunities within the institution for research and sabbaticals, which does help. Art schools as supportive communities of artists is still being developed.

So why did art schools get absorbed into universities?
It was part of the government's educational policy. The only independent art schools now are private. There is a big difference between the old art school system and the current one. There certainly is a huge interest in reviving that ethos uncluttered by current Quality and huge administrative demands.

What are the benefits and drawbacks of each system?
They talk about 'the good old days' but in many ways it wasn't. My experience of being a student then was dreadful compared to what it is like now, certainly in relation to power! I am so jealous of students these days. The system is clear and they know what they're taking on board. They have control to a certain extent and they know how to be students and what the relationship is. Students are in a working relationship with the teaching staff – we work together.

The 'good old days' were when a student was totally powerless! My own experience was of an incredibly sexist culture. As far as I know there were always more female students studying art yet I was always taught by men. There wasn't a woman in fine art teaching at Saint Martins when I was there and it was very much dominated by that sexism.

Yet on the other hand the old art school system really did have a very different personality; I do have a pang of regret when I here my students speak of it as 'Uni'.

So if you fit in with the staff you did well?
Yes. And there were no criteria for what made good work either. It was mostly a matter of guessing at what would be approved of. Constructive criticism and feedback was absolutely not there.

So now things have been standardised to allow for proper and equal tutorials etc?
Yes but that's a nightmare too of course, this whole management structure we have now can be horrific! But there are now guidelines, structures and procedures in place to make things run better and fairer. We also have a tutorial and attendance policy. However, all of these are meaningless and a hindrance unless they make absolute sense to the student and to the tutor. I'm all for making a fair and equal system, I hate the old culture of favouritism and elitism.

As staff we have a relationship with students where we are negotiating what we're teaching and how we're teaching all of the time. One thing I've done since I've been here is to get feedback from the students about what's working, what isn't, how we can improve, how they're experiencing the course etc. That's my job as course director.

I constantly have my ear to the ground and I will try things out as long as it's within what's legal or appropriate.

All universities have to carry out student surveys, the results of which are made known nationally and can be therefore pretty damning if the scores are low – as is that of UAL's. But there may be other reasons for that low score. The University of the Arts is the only university that *just* does art yet the surveys are geared towards other ways of teaching, so we're at a disadvantage there in my opinion.

I'm looking after my team and making sure that these management structures and procedures that do come down don't interfere with our ethos, our philosophy or our approach to what we think we are providing for the students. I think the role of course director is crucial here. What we are doing is made clear to the students and it is working well and we are sticking with it. We're not delivering procedures and regulations, we're not. We have to remember what we're doing in teaching fine art.

Do you think assessments weigh down heavily on students?
They're surprisingly cool about them actually, which I'm glad about.
If you look at the handbook we have frameworks, units, learning outcomes and marking criteria. We 'translate' them for the student or they do it for themselves and we have ongoing discussion about what they all mean. Assessment is ongoing and in a way scrupulous, as in any tutorial; we're addressing the critical and analytical ability of the student and their work. That rigour goes on every day in front of the work and it just translates into this other language to score against at assessment points. Students may have a different language to that but we ask them all the time if they understand. On some level the assessment frameworks are great because they mean we're not assessing students on just one of our personal opinions – it's not how it used to be.

What still does happen though is where the student may get positive feedback from one tutor and perhaps more questioning feedback from another. In the end it's the student who makes the decisions for themselves. It's very important that a student understands that they are never told what to do. Tutorials offer advice and feedback but responsibility for a student's development is their own. If you make that understood at the beginning and the student has the confidence to take on that responsibility for themselves, that is a fantastic tool for them to have.

Hopefully we are sending more confident artists – creative people – out into the world; people who have been able to develop their own individual values and ideas and have a certain amount of confidence about that.

It's about making them aware of their role in their own education? And also of the intentions of the educational formats that they are receiving …
Yes.

Why did you choose to go to art school and why do you think that students go now?
If you were from my generation and background – I came from a lower-middle or working class background – and were academically able, then you were expected to go to university. To choose to go to art school was really questionable back then. I chose to go to art school to get out of that whole fucking class status thing and to get out of all kinds of constraints and expectations. It was not just about being good at art at school or about what job I wanted to choose for life; being an artist was a choice to resist all such expectations.

In those days you chose your life trajectory at an early age and everything was sort of predictable by your academic attainment. You laid out your job for life and as a woman you were married at 21 or otherwise left on the shelf. If you wanted to go on to higher education things like having a year out just weren't done. You went straight from school or else you didn't have another chance. There are different choices now being made for life and at different ages and I've noticed that people who didn't go to art school originally are coming back now as mature students.

As to why students choose to go to art school now I don't know. Prospective students visit the Colleges with their parents – I wouldn't have been seen dead with my parents anywhere near art school! – who are going to pay for them and are asking questions like "What are the prospects for a livelihood?" I have to say "Well it's something like one per cent who make a living out of being a fine artist but most graduates here will go into creative industries".

What would you like to say?
It's not about training for a job. Do parents ask that when their child is doing a geography degree? I'd like to say "Come and do a fine art course because after that you can do anything! You learn to be independent, free-thinking, you become able to make decisions for yourself, to manage your own time, to be creative and self-motivating". Even business schools are trying to encourage creativity in some way, they're all saying they want cre-

ative people! I see that with this huge fee increase business the choice to do a fine art degree is going to be more problematic; certainly those who do insist on that choice will be more determined. There are more directives now coming from the Institution about some kind of job offer at the end of it.

Did you grow up seeing art?
Yes. We were taught well at school and I was always making things, which I loved doing. So when I say I made the decision to go to art school just to be rebellious, that's only a small part of the story. It was only my father saying "you'll never make a living". I think you might be hinting at the advantage of coming from a background where Lacan was talked about over the dining table – I certainly had no such upbringing!

But now the question of a livelihood really is a factor as choosing to study at art school for it's own sake is becoming more and more impossible. My generation had free education and the welfare state. Going to Art School was a life statement about a different possible life to be lived. I'm horrified about the effects of current political repressions.

It was all free?
Absolutely! We were even paid! It was means tested so full grants were available as well as no fees.

Did those grants pay for just tuition or rent also?
Both. The grant available to live on was set at a certain level; your family was means tested; those from better off families were expected to have the shortfall made up by their parent's contribution to that. We all had the same amount of money and we lived on it. And we all had jobs in holidays.

Do you think that there is a difference in the attitudes of those who went to art school then and those who go now?
I don't know whether it's such an issue to escape the constraints or expectations of family background now.

We'll soon see the effects of the likely new fee system; back to the very old days when art schools were for the upper classes?

I absolutely resist and will not use the term 'customer' which is a term this university has started to use for the student! It's the view that we're offering a service. Already students are treating their course as a commodity that they are purchasing i.e. if they don't fancy the goods they can return them; that they are buying a qualification. That relationship just makes it impossible. I cannot stomach that and I would be out of here like a shot!

Are technical skills and workshops supported and valued here?
Technical skills are usually no longer the basic grounding for a fine art education. At Open Days for the course I often get asked about this as though it's a failing and told especially that we should be providing life- drawing classes. It's not that we don't value skills; it's rather that we choose not to base any of our teaching or instruction around their acquisition. We don't start from the teaching of technical skills; students acquire them as needed and our workshops and technicians are fantastic at Chelsea. The ability to manipulate materials is essential.
Let's give an example of a crit with students: Someone is presenting a piece of work that has got nails sticking out of it. We might ask "Is that just shabby craftsmanship or is it actually necessary to an understanding of the work?" So here a student could either say, "Yeah, it's a total failure because I didn't know how to hammer a nail in" or they could say that it is intentional. Even if it's the first, that might then be what makes the work become interesting. It's trashily made; it has become interesting – or not.

So part of the discussion around approaching the artwork is the correct or appropriate use of skills to realise the work. It has to have a physical presence in the world and has to be made and that takes a certain knowledge or acquisition of skills. You could of course use the 'readymade' or have a concept realised by a specialist technician. That process interrupts the presumption that skills are the premise for making work.

This is sometimes quite tragic for students. For those who go to art school because they're good at drawing or whatever, that can be really tragic. They may have been advised to go to art school because they were good at drawing and not much else. They might be better on a skills-based course and one where briefs are set.

But I don't want to trash skills or technical ability. I think a good art school has a balance of technical and academic teaching.

Many technicians have teaching certificates now even if some of our academics don't. The teaching experienced in the workshops might be more time intensive i.e. the student gets more time with the technician than they do with their academic teacher, but there is a difference. Let's take this thing in the crit. The student may have had an idea in their head and gone to the wood technician because they wanted it made in wood. They'd have taken some drawings and would have been helped on a technical basis to realise it. If a work they want to make really demands some technical skills before they can begin to formulate their ideas, they'd have to be learnt and possibly the more proficient they are at that skill, the better work they'll make. Saying that, in some areas, certainly digital skills like film and video, art schools are outstripped by the expertise of those industries.

But some art production can rely on no technical skills whatsoever. Some conceptual work can be far more brilliant than an amazingly immaculately produced object.

Do you think that this latter 'thought led' type of art production is favoured in art colleges now – or at least framed that way? Whilst what you say makes sense, I wonder sometimes if the lack of instruction of technical skill, together with the visible emphasis on academic teaching and discussion, leads students to feel more comfortable or feel that they should be making more conceptually orientated work?

OK you make a good point and that often is the scenario yes. Because this is a dilemma and because I think students feel a bit intimidated by that, I say to them "Look. What do you like doing? What are you good at? If it's knitting, knit! Base your artwork around what you love to do". Everyone should be encouraged to do what they feel confident and good at.

Do you think it's hard to bring concept and technical proficiency together?
I think it's an issue at the starting point but then the basis of our first year of teaching is 'Experimentation and Exploration'. We use those two words deliberately. So maybe students spend time in the workshops or maybe their challenge is to think about other ways of doing things and realise why they're doing them. Thinking and making are bound up together. A large percentage of all students who go to art school come in as painters because that's what secondary education has taught them to do and not necessarily how to think.

At open day when I'm fielding that question about skills, people say "Is it true then that if we're painters we shouldn't be coming to Chelsea?" Because we don't have pathways I have to really deal with that question. My answer is "Look, we don't have pathways, no painting or sculpture courses, but if you come in here as a painter and you say you're a painter and it's obvious you're a painter then you will paint!" But painting practice is wide. You'd certainly be challenged about which is an appropriate medium to explore your ideas with; if it's painting ...

How do you select students?
We take students because we think there's something particular about their own motivation evident in the portfolio, which is usually confirmed at interview with the student. Many prospective students put in about three life drawings and they're either demonstrating skills or demonstrating how well they can interpret set briefs.

Different art colleges have different emphases on what they think will make a good student and we only have a few minutes to interview them, if we do interview them. It's very difficult to select by portfolio only; I am a great believer in allowing the student to represent themselves at a face-to-face interview where they have the opportunity to articulate a knowledge and understanding of their own work and a capacity for independent thinking and also to demonstrate their self-motivation which is so very important in fine art. This year there was a big change in the admissions process. The first choice system was scrapped, and so five-times as many students applied.

You said your course is not divided into disciplines. Can I ask you then what your course philosophy is and why you made the decision to not do that?
We have that statement in the handbook. Our approach to fine art practice is that whatever the student presents as an artwork – is art. It may be bad art, but it *is* art. One of the biggest hurdles may be to break down presumptions of what the student thinks an artwork looks like. It's very simplistic to categorise artwork by it's medium – that's already putting up a division. There are some points when that is useful and important and we do have groups that talk about painting, film, or performance etc. But at this level, it is very necessary and much more fruitful to approach the art work not only in terms of what it's made of but also in terms of what the art work does in the world, how it operates, how we encounter it.

Was it your decision to run a broad-based course then?
Yes. There were three pathways when I took over as course director but I changed it. It was a difficult decision to phase the pathways out but I thought it was important. It didn't mean that the same student wouldn't come here. It also didn't mean that they'd be taught by a different set of tutors, have different locations, technicians and it didn't mean that they couldn't be taught by somebody from another team. There was an exclu-

sive, very competitive and very snobbish attitude between the rankings of painting, sculpture and so on before we brought them together.

We put students haphazardly into groups whatever their practice. So a student might bring in a painting and it might be necessary – but we certainly don't do it for the hell of it – to say in conversation "Had you thought that this might be more effective in 3D? Or, would it be more effective if you added another element like film?" The point is that that question can arise and it's as simple as that. This happens also when the student starts to think critically about the concerns and issues that underpin their practice.

Students, as I mentioned earlier, who have come in at a young age because they were good at something like painting, often introduce themselves as: 'a painter'. The key question for us to think about as staff then, is: Is that label limiting? Or are we posing an unnecessary challenge to the student's belief about what they want to do by asking them if they've cosidered other mediums?

That's the crux of the argument really isn't it?
It is.

Our teaching really focuses on enabling the student to start to think critically about what the artwork does and to think about the best way for them to be able to express their ideas. They may choose to work with a combination of different materials; we do think this approach mirrors a lot of contemporary practices.

Does thinking come through making or does making come through thinking?
Absolutely both. But everyone's different. Sometimes it's necessary to just keep slogging away with your 'stuff' in the studio until it starts to make sense; other ways of working may depend on clarifying ideas so researching issues and rethinking approaches may be more appropriate. That's also the importance of the theoretical element of the course where they are asked to consider the context for their own work.

But then surely it's also about enjoying making the work?
That certainly comes with confidence. We do say to students to make use of the skills they're good at and enjoy making. If they love to knit, then knit!

I tell students that they are the next generation of artists and that they will determine what that's going to be. We can't demonstrate that to them and we can't tell them. We engage in the critical and analytical skills they need and negotiate with them what they're doing. We guide them even though they may reject our advice totally. But the art students benefit from that situation as they are learning to make their own decisions.

That's interesting because students usually arrive on a course expecting to be taught something.
Yes and that's very hard. First years weep!

But I haven't said we don't teach them anything – we certainly do!

We do teach loads and loads of skills and the skills we do teach are how to be critical, how to conduct research and develop analytical skills. We equip students with the language to do that. Our art theory and a lecture programme introduces discourses and practices that we think they need to be familiar with. Lectures, theory seminars, practical workshops and lots of elements of the course are actually taught and even the seminar groups are led with very clear guidelines. Students are expected to draw upon all of this knowledge and get their head into things that interest them. Learning how to put a nail in properly will not necessarily turn you into an artist.

The crucial thing is how they then use that. There's no parrot learning here. Some students say 'My tutor told me this should be blue and not red' and they will follow that like an instruction. Some students might defer to the tutors knowledge and authority that a tutor's opinion is 'correct' and best for them.

Back to the seminar situation where we are all looking at a block of wood with nails sticking out of it. The emphasis for the seminar is that all the students in the group should start to engage and contribute to developing a discussion around it, yet a typical reaction that might then occur is "I am silent because I have no opinion". It's not no *opinion,* it's no *tools.* Students shouldn't feel embarrassed. It's: "I don't know what to think or how to think". That then may be a failing of ours to teach them to start that process. Maybe that is a skill of the leader, to teach them how to think. So we demonstrate: "OK, how do we think it is made?" Students may find that easier to engage with: "Oh I do have an opinion on that". Then: "What are your feelings in relation to it?" "Actually it makes me scared", or "It's deadly boring" or "I think it's a piece of shit" or "I think it's fabulous", or – more to the point: "I don't really see why the nails are sticking out!" You've got an opinion. Sometimes it can get personal or too offensive and we have to put a halt to that.

So they too are skills. They are not technical skills but they are skills in how to make judgements. In order to progress through your own practice you need to be able to make judgements about your own practice. For instance asking yourself "Is that working?" or "Why have I decided to put that there?" Those are critical skills that you're not just born with. It's hard work.

What was really interesting there was when you said "It's not that I don't have an opinion, it's I don't have the tools". I think that's it. Reading art is a difficult thing to do and if you've not necessarily grown up looking at art and then you're thrown into a context where you're supposed to be able to read it and it seems that everyone else can…

It can also get in the way if you get too caught up in that. At the beginning when students first come in they might have a presumption about what the artwork should look like and we have to knock that on the head. It's almost better to have a blank canvas because too much knowledge is often prejudicial to their engagement with something. It's a judgement in a negative way. Its "I don't like it". Typically it might be something that's pornographic or political, insulting or culturally difficult.

I didn't see contemporary art until I was 19. It makes you shy to give an opinion because you think you can't.
Confidence.

When I first came to Goldsmiths there were people in convenors who'd talk a lot and show that they have this huge knowledge …

Hell. Very intimidating. That's very negative. I think it's up to the skill of a good teacher to create a situation in which the discussion itself becomes the focus and to encourage the generosity of the group to contribute. That's about leading and directing the discussion. I don't know what's being displayed there. It takes a lot for another student to stand up and say "You're talking a load of fucking rubbish, meaningless to me sorry. I don't know what an earth you're saying! What is this display of knowledge? Could you please translate?"

You can't really do that can you?

No. Nobody wants to admit that they don't know!

But is that other person saying that they do know? Is this about knowledge? I think structures for teaching are very important. At Chelsea we have fairly small seminar groups led by a tutor who stays with them for a year; during this time the group does start to trust each other. The skill of the tutor in leading this group is very important; it's a hard job.

Art is portrayed as a knowledge game isn't it?

That's bad. For me that's just bad.

Liking it is one thing, understanding is something else. Like anything, the more you know about something the more pleasurable it is. But not to know can be liberating.

ANDREW BANNISTER

Andrew Bannister is head of Fine Art Sculpture at the independently run
City & Guilds of London Art School. We met in late October 2010 at his
flat in Deptford, South East London.

Can you outline your role at City & Guilds?
Since 2005 I've been working at City & Guilds of London Art School, an
independent art school based in Kennington, between Oval and Elephant
and Castle on Kennington Park Road. I manage the sculpture department
there and much of my job is taken up with organising the day-to-day
operations of the department as well as with teaching on the BA and MA
Fine Art courses.

The Fine Art BA undergraduate course has two pathways, painting
and sculpture, on which students study full-time. We also have some postgraduate diploma provision where students can study one year full-time or
two years part-time.

I think the school is interesting because there are a number of courses
and departments all based in a relatively small location. The school occu-
pies a number of terraced houses facing onto the main road that date back
to the Georgian era, and a building with large studios that was built in the
late nineteenth century.

What are the different departments?
There is a Conservation department, where students learn the practical
skills and technical knowledge involved in the field of conservation – primarily of sculptural objects. Also there is a Historic Carving course, which
is largely concerned with teaching stone and wood carving skills and techniques relevant to replication carving practices that are mostly linked to

the heritage industries. There is a foundation course, which has grown a lot in the last few years and has about 40-45 students. Fine art is located in the same building as the foundation course – and that's where the sculpture department is.

How long did you say you'd been working at the college for?
I've been in the post of head of sculpture since 2005 but previous to that I had worked there since 2002, working for a day or two a week on the sculpture pathway.

Did you study art yourself?
Yes. I did my foundation course at Croydon College, in Selhurst Road. That's now where the Brit School is, the Performing Arts school set up by Richard Branson and others in the late 1980s. My course was located there for a few years until it moved to the college's main site in central Croydon. It was a fairly broad-based foundation course and while I was there I chose to specialise in fine art.

I then went to Trent Polytechnic – which now has the name of Nottingham Trent University – to do a degree in fine art, which I completed in 1990. Following that, I had a year out during which I stayed in Nottingham. I spent that year doing various part-time jobs and getting a portfolio together to apply for postgraduate study. I applied to just one place, Chelsea College of Art, and was accepted onto the Sculpture MA course where I studied from 1991-1992. At that time the sculpture department was located in Manresa Road, off of the Kings Road.

Just out of curiosity, why did you decide to go to Nottingham to study – especially as you were from London, a place full of so many good art schools?
That was a long time ago and I'm not sure if my memory stretches that far back! I remember that I went to a few places to look around: Winchester,

Canterbury and Nottingham. I just felt that Nottingham seemed like the most suitable course for me to apply to. It was a broad-based fine art course and at that point [1987] there were relatively few courses in the UK that were like that. You didn't have to choose which media area you would focus on in the first year and, in fact, you could quite easily go through all three years without specialising and work across different media areas. In a sense, that was something that the college prided itself on. Also, I wanted to get out of London and I liked Nottingham as a city so I decided that it was the place for me to go to.

Interestingly enough, many of the tutors that I spoke to at Nottingham when I studied there felt that Goldsmiths was the course that was most similar to theirs in terms of the general ethos of cross-media thinking and practice.

Did you do any teacher training?
No I didn't do any training at all. Nowadays though, if you are appointed as a new *permanent* member of staff in a university and have less than three years of teaching experience you need to undergo training in your first year of employment – this came in a number of years after I got my first teaching job. When I started teaching it was in a part-time, sessional capacity. Back then, I think that it was largely a matter of being asked back to teach at the college where you'd studied.

What made you decide to go on to teach?
Actually I was asking myself this the other day. When did I *know* or when did I decide I wanted to get involved in teaching? I think that by the third year of the degree course at Nottingham I'd more or less figured out that that was what I was going to do, but I didn't gather any teaching experience whilst I was on the course. There were people on the course who were involved in community teaching and stuff but I never did anything like that. I think that teaching was something I just felt drawn to do.

There wasn't an exact point when I said to myself, "Yes, this is what I'm doing for my career," as I wasn't really thinking about a career at this stage. Remember, this was at a time when very little discussion took place on degree courses about career pathways or development. There was no advice given about what career you might pursue after graduating… which is very different now. Nowadays, on most courses there is a degree of emphasis on 'professional development' and what are called 'transferable skills'.

Do you think all art colleges should have a professional development programme?
Yes, I think it's important. But I also think – and this is, I guess, a liberal arts education viewpoint – that there are things you learn during three years of study that are important and even though they might not necessarily have a *direct* application, they are vital to a rounded educational experience.

Do you have a professional development programme at City & Guilds?
Yes. There are a series of Professional Practice seminars that take place in the spring and summer term, primarily aimed at third years and MA students. These are delivered by people working in the fine art arena like artists, gallerists and writers, and cover issues that broadly relate to how students might continue working as artists upon leaving college.

Do you think art is a subject that can be taught?
Yes I do. I think it's important to impart subject knowledge to students, as well as knowledge of certain ways or approaches to making things and certain approaches to thinking about art. Those are the three crucial things that need to be passed on and that is why I think art *is* something that can be taught.

I was looking at the City & Guilds of London Art School website earlier today and there is a passage that reads, "We prioritise skill-based teaching and value tradition as both historic and ongoing." Could you unpack this a bit?
In terms of the skills-based emphasis there are a number of ways of looking at that.

One of the key features of the school lies in its stress on the importance of making things, and I think that this always involves some level of skill. The emphasis is not so much on learning craft skills to a really high degree and then perfecting them – it's more to do with an approach that prioritises hands-on making and thinking through making.

There are areas of refinement in terms of those skills. For instance, if you're learning how to make moulds and cast objects, we believe that there is a lot to be gained from learning to do that yourself rather than saying, "Here's my idea, I'll hand it over to a technician who will then give it back to me when it's done." From the time spent making and learning about the nature of the materials, their properties and their possibilities, one inevitably starts to think about the creative application of those processes and how this links in with one's practice.

Those are all things I'd define as being really central to what we call 'skills-based' teaching.

So in this sense then the word skill is linked to a craft or technique-based process?
Yes. I think there are different ways of thinking about craft but in a way it's largely about an engagement with particular processes of making and of getting to really know what those are and gaining some control and mastery over them.

I don't see what we do though as being traditionalist in a sense of prioritising technique over and above everything else, as is the case with forms of conservative practice where the work is largely a demonstration of technique in a traditional idiom. Rather, what we try to do is place an equal emphasis on the activities of making and thinking about the critical context in an intelligent a way as possible. I don't see these things as being exclusive from each other.

Do you think your course differs a lot from the other London art courses?
While all courses differ from each other in certain ways, as far as I can tell there are certain things that are shared. Other courses that I know of *are* increasingly placing an emphasis on students directly making things in their first year in order to get them to apply themselves practically, rather than sitting around and thinking, "What shall I make?" In other words, they encourage people to get involved in the processes of making and thinking creatively, rather than getting too involved in a process of questioning or working purely conceptually right from the start.

Am I right in thinking that in the first year you have a series of projects?
Yes, and these run for the whole of the first year. Through these projects we introduce students to various ways of making artworks and the skills and techniques that this involves.

Can you give an example?
In the first term we have a module that runs in both the painting and sculpture pathways, titled The Body in Context, which contains several project elements. In one of the projects, students make a work in response to visual information they gather relating to the human body and its representation within art and science. The emphasis is as much on the research and information gathering processes as it is on the actual hands-on making of things.

Also, throughout the year we include inductions to workshops. These usually take one or two days each and involve students acquiring basic technical skills and applying them in the context of the projects they're working on. So the first day of a project might be mostly technical, in terms of looking at different materials, properties and techniques, and the second day will involve making something that relates to the brief of the project. So as well as being about acquiring skills, we are interested in getting students thinking about the creative application of techniques right from the start.

Do you think that's important? It's as if by doing so you're saying, "It's OK to go and use different materials." This way students get to know how to use the workshops and can be confident in doing so – so even if they don't choose to work in that way they know that they can.
That's right.

Whereas I guess, if you're not given that opportunity to try things out you may not use the workshop facilities, even though they're there. That may be through fear – conscious or not – of the perception that it's not the 'done thing' or whatever?
Yes. I think that even if students don't get on with a particular material or process after a workshop induction session and don't ever use it again, they will hopefully have acquired some experience which might be useful in the future, in terms of their general understanding of the properties of materials, and the potential applications of techniques and processes.

It seems that on the whole, there isn't so much of an emphasis within fine art courses now on operating these material/technique induction workshops. Some people have suggested that this perhaps leads towards more of a 'thinking' based practice.

I have two questions. First is do you agree with this suggestion? And second, if so do you think this move was triggered by economic or pedagogic reasons?
I think there are a number of factors here. A lot of it relates to the economics of the situation. For instance, having increasingly large student year groups would make it quite difficult to manage 'hands-on' workshops,

and by 'hands-on' I mean a workshop that is about more than just, "This is a drill," or, "This is a nail." Workshops that delve into more detail and open up more of a creative space are difficult to run with a large cohort of students.

I also think that the pedagogical side *has* had an impact. Over the last twenty years within art schools – and I'm aware that this is a broad generalisation – there has been a shift away from the idea of art as an activity that primarily involves the use of craft skills towards one that is more located in ideas and concepts. I think there are many reasons for this, such as the shifts taking place in the theoretical landscape as well as the context of contemporary art. It could be argued that within some quarters, the idea of skills-based teaching was regarded as somewhat reactionary. There were political reasons for this, where a certain generation of teachers felt that art's priorities should lie elsewhere. So there was, perhaps, a move away from a model of teaching that focused on techniques and skills towards one that was more focused on critical and theoretical issues. I myself became aware of this kind of shift in the discourse around art during my time at art school in the late eighties and early nineties.

If that was a politicised reaction made at a particular time for a particular reason, has that model remained intact because of a continuation of that political impetus – or is it just a hangover that hasn't since been rethought?
I think that in the late eighties or nineties there were a lot of arguments going on around the need to have a more theorised basis for practice. Perhaps some of the ambitions there were generational – a certain generation of tutors in their twenties and thirties, trying to displace the model of education they had which was set very much within a Modernist framework. It goes back to the battles that took place within art schools in the seventies as well.

What battles?

Broadly speaking, battles relating to the idea of radicalism within art and the notion of committed, politicised forms of practice versus ones rooted in traditional understandings or Modernist conceptions of art. But that's another area.

Do you think theory weighs down on students? Do you think the tendency is for them to think, "I should be making through thinking," rather than the reverse?

I think the challenge is to look at both of those things and not with the view that one cancels out the other. I agree with the opinion that there can be a situation where if students are engaged in what is a largely cerebral activity, it can begin to cancel out other avenues that might be interesting to explore.

Something I have in the past found difficult to deal with is the situation where students get into a state of creative paralysis, saying, "I can't make any work because I haven't got any ideas." I think that it would be better if they just got on and did something, whether it's taking some photographs or making an object with available materials; trying to get beyond that idea that art is a rational activity and a matter of, "Here's my idea and here's how I'm going to execute it."

So essentially I think that what *we're* trying to do is to get around this problem by saying that perhaps it's better to shoot first and ask questions later. Then, once there is something there, we can subject it to some sort of critical appraisal. And that may not be to do with theory as such; it may take the form of a general discussion around what it was the student was seeking to do and what the object they've made actually does. To what extent does it reflect or communicate their intentions? Then you can open up other questions about the wider context of practice, how artworks are interpreted and so on.

In terms of the day-to-day running of your course, how does it work and where does the education – or teaching – take place?
On the undergraduate sculpture pathway that I'm in charge of, we have a relatively small cohort, or it would at least be considered small by some. We have a maximum of around five or six students per year.

The first year is structured around a series of projects, whilst the second and third year students work on their own self-defined work. We try to organise the staffing in such a way that there is a member of staff teaching on the pathway each day. There are a range of visiting tutors who work on average two or three days a month. I'm in for two and a half days a week, and I have a colleague who is usually in for around two days a week.

As well as the scheduled tutorials, there is a lot of informal contact. Some of the student-tutor discussions relate to practical issues. A student might ask a tutor in passing, "How do you do this?" or, "How might I find out about this artist?" or ,"What do you think of this?" Or it might be some other discussion relating to art and wider culture. We're able to offer this kind of informal contact, which we regard as very important to the overall feel of the course.

The second and third years have two tutorials with their personal tutor per term. They are usually about an hour long and are not exactly review points, but function as a context in which tutors talk in depth with the student about how their work is evolving, what key issues they need to think about and so on. Students can also supplement this with tutorials from visiting tutors, which they can sign up for throughout the year.

Over the last year or so we've also added a series of seminars, about two per term that the students are required to attend. They are essentially a kind of group tutorial with students from both the painting and sculpture pathways and each time there is a different emphasis. This term we ran one on the themes or subjects of the students' work and in the following session we looked at how each student's research related to their practice.

Because in sculpture we have a relatively small group of students it is quite easy to get together for informal group tutorials and we do that once or twice a term.

Did you say there are just five students per year on your course?
Yes. Though currently it's smaller than that. In the second and third year we have two students and in the first year we have four. So that group discussion also goes some way towards compensating for the small number of students we have.

Can I ask why there are so few students?
Relative to other degree courses the sculpture provision at City & Guilds has always been fairly small. In a way it takes me back to when I first started studying. Although at Trent Polytechnic it was a broad-based course, invariably you found that whilst there were a certain number who chose to experiment, people largely fell into one of three categories: sculpture; painting; and what was then called mixed media. I remember that when I was in my first year at Trent Polytechnic there were probably about three or four students specialising in sculpture, so in a way it's interesting to compare the current situation with the one that existed when I began studying 24 years ago.

How many students are on the painting pathway?
It varies between about 15-20 students per year. So it is significantly larger than sculpture but it is also fairly small.

Do you specify that you can only take a certain number of students onto the course?
Well currently it would be difficult to accommodate more than six people per year and so five or six is about the target.

Is that because of the number of staff or because of the space?
There are spatial limitations at the college and if we had a larger number of students electing to study sculpture we'd have to negotiate for more space with the other departments in the college.

City & Guilds is an independent school isn't it?
Yes it is. Although in the mid 1990s, the fine art course was re-launched as a validated undergraduate degree course – that is, a course validated by a partner institution, in this case Birmingham City University.

So one can't presumably just decide, "We're going to open up a school and award degrees." Like you said, it has to be validated by another degree awarding institution …?
That's right. Prior to the mid 1990s the college used to award a diploma certificates rather than degrees. There are other art schools in existence that only offer diplomas and they're purely independent and have no connection with any other validating institution.

Can I ask how much the fees are?
The fees for the undergraduate course are around £7,500 a year.

Wow. I mean my immediate reaction was to think, "That's a lot!" But that's also likely to be the price of state funded higher education now isn't it? In fact, yours might even be cheaper?!
Who knows? There's a lot of speculation that universities are going to be able to set their tuition fee levels wherever they want. Currently it's looking like universities might set their fees anywhere from £6,000 plus. But Nick Clegg seems to be indicating that this might not happen.

[This interview took place one month before the vote was passed to raise the cap on tuition fees to a maximum of £9,000 in November 2011.]

That raises the question of what will happen. With this current government a lot of institutions are looking at significant funding cuts.

So because City & Guilds is independent, does that mean there is little or no interference from the government as to how you must run your course?
You mean, as there's no public money is there a necessity to conform to certain government policies …?

Yes. We speculated earlier that courses might make choices about what they do and do not offer based on economics. Without such constraints and with small student numbers, can your course therefore run exactly the way it wants to?
Well not entirely. I think in terms of the ethos of prioritising both craft skills and an interest in questions of critical context, yes, that's up to us. But we do have to conform to some government-based requirements in terms of the structuring of the courses. That's what the validation is about.

So things like credit ratings for each level of the course and also the adoption of a modular structure…they're both things that we are required to do because of our partnership with Birmingham City University. There are also other things we're required to do, like having external examiners and annual monitoring processes. But it's fine. We've been able to retain our ethos without significantly altering the way we do things.

What is your policy and responsibility as a school in terms of widening participation? Do you award bursaries?
There is some money allocated for bursary support. Currently it is reserved for students who are already here who've been able to pay for their first year themselves. They can apply at the end of the first or second year for some support for their second or third year, which might cover up to half of their fees.

We also have some awards relating to competitions, such as the Beckwith Award, where students in either the first or second year of the sculpture pathway submit a proposal for a study visit to an international destination of their choice with the aim of researching aspects of the culture of that country, or techniques and processes that are particular to the sculptural traditions of that country. This year the award was won by a second year student who travelled to Mozambique to research African art and wood-carving traditions. He was given £1,000 to cover his travel and subsistence costs and he also received a terms fees.

What's the difference between working for an independent art school and a state funded university? Why did you choose to work here?
Primarily the differences are to do with the size of the college and its general ethos.

At the college there is a foundation course, the conservation and carving courses and the fine art BA and MA. All in all there are about two hundred students, including part-time and full-time students. And that's the key difference I think, that it is relatively small. There is also a larger amount of one-to-one contact between students and tutors than at many other colleges.

Currently we have a staff-student ratio of around one to eight. It's very different to the current models in universities where there is a greater emphasis on students having a large degree of responsibility for their own learning. I'd argue that within higher education over the last ten years there has been a shift away from the idea of the tutor being someone who imparts knowledge to students. In many institutions there is a sense that rather than teaching students deep subject knowledge, you teach students study skills so that they can acquire knowledge on their own. The idea of the tutor as a custodian of knowledge is becoming quite an unfashionable one really.

Is this 'independent learning' strategy a nicer way of saying that there aren't enough resources?
Well I tend towards that view. Having said that, I think independent learning *is* important. It's too simplistic to say that you're the tutor and they're

the student and they just learn from you. I wouldn't want that to be the case. But I do think that this has largely come about as a result of the financial situation that British universities have been in over recent years.

It's definitely possible to see the argument from both sides ...
Yes and it's definitely about achieving a balance. You've got to have both. Saying that, I definitely do think that the scales have tipped too much to one side.

How do you think art college differs now from when you were at college?
I think there are a number of ways of looking at this. Comparing 1987 when I began my degree course and now, there is a huge difference it seems in terms of the level of public interest in contemporary art. And that's definitely changed the way that students think about the subject and perhaps also their motivations for studying it as well.

When I was a student there was little emphasis placed on the idea of a career after art school. It wasn't really discussed much. Perhaps there was more of a romantic perception of art – that you were an artist, not because you wanted a career as an artist, but because you had to be! We also recognised and it was made clear to us, that only a certain number of people would leave art school and make a living out of making art.

When you were studying did you have to pay fees?
Like everyone else studying for a first degree at the time, my fees were paid for. I had practically a full maintenance grant for the three years of the course. When I went to Chelsea though that wasn't the case. I had a grant to cover the fees but not living costs so I stayed at home with my parents that year.

You mentioned that students' motivations for studying art may have changed and that they now seem to anticipate a career in art at the end of their period of study. One reason for this might be the proliferation of the art market in recent years, the other could be students hoping to get some kind of return for the money they've spent on fees and living costs – particularly those from low income backgrounds … What do you think?

I think that partly because of the endless revisiting of the so-called YBA phenomenon and the increase in the public interest in contemporary art, it does look to many people like art has become a viable career option. When I was a student it didn't really enter my head. But art schools at that time seemed to operate more as zones of dissent, where art was regarded as a form of non-alienated labour. This all changed significantly from the point that art schools became required to be far more accountable to government.

Do you encourage students to see some of the smaller galleries in London as well as the larger ones?

Yes we do.

And do you think that influences their work in any way?

I think it depends on the student. I think you'll find that it does if the student is perhaps more ambitious or curious about art activity taking place outside the mainstream. The students I've taught over the years who have gone on to get involved in the art world or gone on to further study, have been the people who were really keen on their undergraduate courses to find out what's going on 'outside' of the Sunday colour supplement view of art in Britain.

Perhaps when I was a student I fell into that category. I wanted to find out about what was new and interesting. I spent a lot of time in the late 1980s trekking around the East End visiting gallery spaces that were then regarded as experimental and cutting edge.

Do they hope to emulate what they see?
I guess. We take them out for study visits from time-to-time and we go beyond the West End. There are people in the staff body who are very plugged into the context of artist run spaces and small, younger galleries. To many students who come here in the first year, it's very exciting to start looking at these spaces they didn't know existed.

Why do you encourage them to look?
It's to do with looking at new art that is exhibited before what might be termed the 'filtration process' takes place, critical or otherwise; before things enter the mainstream market or museum context. Also, if you go around many of the East End spaces you can talk to people who are actively involved in the making and presentation of new work. It's rather different from walking around a West End gallery space or museum. It's a world that is closer perhaps to the ethos of art schools, rather than the ethos of the commercial art world.

In terms of assessing work on a course and assessing work in a gallery by an artist you've never ever seen before, do you employ similar value criteria when making judgements about the work? And what are those criteria, what's the process?
This is a very interesting question and something that often occurs to me when I'm looking around shows or at art in general. I think that the criteria for determining what 'good work' is, or what 'quality' is are complex and difficult to define, and these criteria vary in different contexts. Also, in an educational setting the process of evaluating a student's work and their progress isn't just focused on the object or final work. You're assessing a student's learning and whether what they make is reflecting *their* understanding of what it is they are doing and the wider context of practice. It's also standard practice in most art schools that as well as producing art works, students are required to produce supplementary material and documentation that gets taken into consideration in assessment contexts.

On the whole I think that it's usually fairly easy to tell by looking at the work and the supplementary material how successful they have been. It's not always an easy process and often there are differences of opinion in teams of assessors, which then have to be thrashed out to reach a consensus.

In a degree show situation a student might not have pulled it off in terms of their show but their work up to that point and the commitment to their studies might have been very good. So you have to evaluate them in terms of their studies as a whole.

So how does that process compare to you walking into a gallery space showing work by an unknown artist?
I think that if you have a knowledge of the language of art and its histories, it *is* possible to gauge whether the work is successful or not. It is of course also important to factor in questions of personal taste, bias and preference that play a part in this process.

What do you think the purpose of a degree show is and does everyone's work fit into that context?
It represents a recognisable goal for the work that students work towards. With sculpture it's particularly important because sculpture is frequently difficult to show and only comes to a point of completion when it is displayed. So for the sculpture students it's good to have something they can plan and work towards.

There is also the bonus of having your work seen by your peers and the public, of getting feedback, of maybe selling some work or getting opportunities to exhibit.

Out of curiosity, did you go to see art when you were growing up?
Both of my parents were involved in education, and they nurtured my creative interests. When I was about fifteen or sixteen I became really inter-

ested in art and from that point regularly visited the Tate Gallery. I also remember clearly the shows at the Royal Academy in the mid to late 1980s, particularly the large survey exhibitions of twentieth century German and British art; these had a big impact on me at the time.

LOUIS NIXON

Louis Nixon is head of the School of Fine Art at Kingston University, a position he has held since 2005. We met in a room above the on-campus Stanley Picker Gallery in November 2010, a week before the first of the student marches against the coalition government's proposal to raise the cap on tuition fees.

Please can you outline the course you teach on and what your role is?
I am the head of the School of Fine Art, a role that I took on in 2005. I oversee the academic management of the school and all of its courses. I teach across most courses in the school, the courses are BA Fine Art, BA Photography, BA Art Performance and Digital Media, MA Art and Space, MA European Art Practice, the PhD programme and now also a new MA called MA Fine Art with Certificate of Learning and Teaching.

What's that?
It's a course where students study for a fine art MA qualification and they also get a postgraduate teaching certificate. It's proven to be quite popular.

What did you do beforehand?
Before that I was a part-time lecturer at the University of Greenwich, teaching art to architects. I also taught part-time at the University of Westminster, part-time here, and was a visiting lecturer at a number of art schools across England.

Can you talk a bit about the history the school?
Around 1899 that little building there ...

(Points out of the window of the room we are in to a building just opposite)

... was set up as a technical college. It was a place for local people in the Surrey and Kingston area to do art and craft. Around 1962 that college split into a college of Further Education (FE) and a college of technology. In 1992 it became a university. Lots of the staff that came to work here then were focussed on – and thereby so was the course – the disciplines of painting, sculpture and intermedia. Since then, the course has become a generic fine art course whereby students are encouraged to work across disciplines. Also, there are now new BA courses in the school and there has been an expansion of taught postgraduate courses and fine art PhDs.

The ethos of the place when it was established was very much about teaching creative skills to local people. Once it became a university though, I think it started to fit more with wider university agendas.

Are those agendas less concerned with the provision of taught skills?
There's always this argument about skills in art education that I don't think will ever go away. When I took over as head of the school I was very much against teaching skills.

Why?
Because there are so many skills you would need to teach that you wouldn't ever get on to anything else. My feeling is that fine art has to be an ideas-based activity whereby the skills you need depend on the kind of idea that you're trying to develop; and we've got incredible resources here for supporting that way of working. For instance, if you want to make a broadcast-quality TV documentary then there's a place here that you can do that.

If you want to record really high-quality sound, you can do that here too. You can make anything here, but we don't teach you how to do it until you need to know.

Are people OK with that? I mean, are students generally confident enough to have an idea, decide they want to work with it in a particular medium and then just go for it?
I think so yes, though obviously that confidence develops throughout the degree course.

We also run projects and inductions in the first year to make the students more comfortable about going into the workshops and comfortable with each other. Perhaps because there are so many students on the course – about two hundred – we noticed that first year students weren't developing the studio culture that I think is so important in fine art education. It's important to get them going, there's nothing worse than sitting in your studio space and endlessly thinking "What am I going to do now?"

Can you say a bit more about the projects you set?
Yes. An example would be one called 'Primal Mud', which was run by the artist Mark Hosking who ordered a ton of clay and simply told the students to work very directly and intuitively with the material. They took it in a number of different directions, which was good for Mark because his work is ceramic based and what happened formed research for him, and it was good for the students because they could learn new skills and talk to other students about what they were doing. We also did a project called Artspectacular, led by Guy Bar Amotz. That was all about making live film and video work. These are projects linked to artists' own research.

Setting projects is quite a big shift from the likes of my own art education. Mine was more, "There's your space, now get on with it!"

Where did you study?
I decided at a very early age that I wanted to go to art school. I did my foundation course at Exeter College of Art and Design and I did painting at Chelsea College of Art and Design from 1984-1987. I then went on to the Slade. It was really interesting at Chelsea because even though I was in a painting subject area, the fourth floor was an open area where students were encouraged *not* to paint. I was with people who were making things and that really suited me.

I think a mistake that students make is to enter onto a degree course thinking, "I am a painter," or, "I am a sculptor." I went in as a painter who didn't really feel happy painting for the first few months, so I was very liberated to realise that I could do other things.

We had really interesting artists teaching us like Roger Ackling, Alan Charlton and Kevin Atherton. It was a really brilliant course, with great tutors, great visiting artists and lots of other activities. I remember that on a Tuesday evening we had a Philosophy class. We could finish in the studio and then go and listen to small seminar discussions with philosophers.

Wow.
Yes, wow. We would also have brilliant musicians coming in at lunchtime like Evan Parker and performing in the lecture theatre. So although we were doing this subject called 'art' we got a real mix of interesting stuff and creative people. Straight after that I went to the Slade to do my MA.

Which MA?
I applied to do mixed media but I ended up in sculpture. I thought the mixed media course would be a bit of paint, bit of glue, a bit of wood …

(Both laugh)

… I didn't realise that it was actually lens-based stuff! I sent in my port-folio and they gave me an interview in the sculpture department. At the interview they said, "Look, we don't think you're right for the mixed media course but you'll be alright in sculpture." So there I went. It turned out fine because you could make whatever you wanted to and it was also a really exciting time to be there.

When I was at Chelsea it was still an independent college and not yet a part of the London Institute. When I was at the Slade, interesting discussions began to develop amongst the staff about fine art research and research is now the big agenda for universities.

Did you receive a grant whilst studying?
Yes. From what I can remember I had all of my fees paid and I had a means-tested maintenance grant. I had money every term to pay for food and subsistence and I also had housing benefit. You could rent a flat and that would be paid for as well. I also had a travel grant.

What was that for?
The government obviously recognised that students would go back and forth to their family home during the course of their degree and so there was money set aside for us to do that two or three times a year.

Surely that's all?
Yes. No! I almost forgot, at the beginning of each term we had a mate-rials allowance. At Chelsea I had £60 to buy paint from the shop. That was quite a lot of money then and you could buy a lot of paint. So it was very do-able.

For me having a big studio on the Kings Road and being amongst in-teresting people making art, was exactly where I wanted to be. Why would you not want that all day every day? Though I didn't have to have a regular job I suppose. A lot of my students now have to fit their degree in around a part-time job.

Is it mainly economics that divides art school experiences then and now do you think? Or is there something else?
Economics does have a massive impact. It has to. I think we'll see that now again. Though it's not just economics, there are moments when lots of different things simply come together.

Such as?
Well back then it wasn't just about art, it was also music and fashion. Lots of things came together in the nineties, making London a very exciting place. I think a lot of it was a result of the creative education being offered by institutions within London at that time – one that I don't think can be mirrored now. I'm not saying that *everything* came out of art school, but certainly that whole 'Cool Britannia' and the regeneration of Shoreditch did. It was a product of young people having the freedom to set their own agendas and be creative in a run down urban area. And developers saw that there was profit to be made.

Do you think that now people are paying for a course there is more of an expectation, or at least a pre-occupation with getting a career at the end?
Yes. Well, we didn't have to think about that so much.

Because it was free? Presumably now one could only afford to not think like that if they have a certain level of financial security?
It helped, yes. If I was going to have ended up with £30,000 – £40,000 worth of debt, that fact would have hung over me and made me very

depressed. It would also have stifled the things I did and changed the decisions that I made.

Though it was the same reality then as now; that having an art education doesn't necessarily mean you'll be an artist or get a job. Lots of students have always gone into related work, or onto other interesting things. The difference is that now people are entering that reality with £40,000 worth of debt, and that really limits your options.

Nowadays there are so many students going through art education, so many courses, and so many galleries. Back then there were very few galleries. When I left the Slade there was Karsten Schubert and Lisson.

That was it?
Yes, but that was good because it meant that we had to set our *own* things up. When I left the Slade I set up this organisation called 'Space Explorations', which ran for about ten years. We set up projects in empty disused spaces and it was exciting; we felt that we could do anything we wanted. There was a recession, there were lots of spaces available, not many artists, not many galleries and so it was a really exciting time to be a young artist.

What made you decide to teach?
Well, both my mum and my dad taught at art school …

(Both laugh)

… So I was exposed at an early age to the art school environment and found it an exciting place to be. It was so free and I felt secure and comfortable, and interested in the other people and how they made art. But when did I know I wanted to teach? I never really wanted to teach!

I just wanted to be an artist and it wasn't until I left art school, after I'd set up Space Explorations and we were doing some projects, that I started getting invited into art schools to talk about my work. I enjoyed talking to other people about their work too and I really got into it. It was a way of inputting back into an environment that I got so much out of myself. It was good job satisfaction and it felt like a worthwhile thing to do.

Did you do any teacher training?
No. Although along the road to where I am now I have had certain points of training. But I think really you learn on the job.

Do you think that art is a subject that can be taught?
Not in the conventional sense, no. You can't teach it like a language or a science because often the answers aren't known and what we're hoping anyway is that students will come up with something far more interesting than we can imagine. I think it's about setting up an environment for something creative to happen and I also think that students' teaching each other is very important.

You *can* teach certain principles though, like how you need to have an idea. You have to have a good idea and you have to find a way of taking that idea out of your head and putting it in the world in front of other people.

It's a complex form of teaching and I do think that it's the hardest subject to learn. I say that to all of my students that this is the hardest degree one can do.

Do you think your philosophy then is more 'making through thinking', than 'thinking through making'?
Yes, though I think both forms of making are valid. You could start with an idea and think through it rigorously or you might equally go into a room, pour a bottle of ink on the floor and something could happen. The latter is certainly the kind of teaching that was taking place in the sixties and seventies, the creation of a situation that students then have to respond to. In either case you have to have the thing in front of you to talk about it.

In a crit?
Yes. Which raises another point about how the physical forms of teaching haven't really changed since then. You've still got the tutorial, the seminar, the artist talk, and the 'crit' as people call it. That's all remained consistent for decades and I wonder if something should change there?

You mentioned that art is one of the most difficult subjects to both teach and learn. Do you think that a lot of the education takes place within the model of the crit, say by osmosis rather than didacticism?
In a seminar situation one develops confidence in being able to communicate and interpret the work collectively, this opens up new and often unexpected understandings and directions for the work to go in.

OK.
When I was at art school I hated talking to people in public and so if there was a crit I would be ill that day. I didn't know what my work was about, how to talk about it and I didn't feel confident standing there. Now though, being in the position I am, I try to build the students' confidence. So the crit here – and I don't even call it a crit, we call it a seminar – is a very supportive environment. Students learn a lot about how to 'be' in the world via the experience of coming into a seminar with an artwork they have created and talking about it.

What's the difference?
In a *crit* you bring work in to be taken apart by other people. But in a *seminar* here, you bring something in and that starts a discussion that is intended to be supportive and developmental, and we would hope that the student has taken the thing apart already.

How big are the crit groups?
Seminar groups …

Sorry!

(Both laugh)

It's OK. I have a problem with the term crit I think because it scared me. Perhaps if it had been described to me as a seminar, so you come in, you have a discussion… I would have probably gone. It's friendlier. Anyway, there are usually about 12-18 people, in a three-hour session with six people given about 30 minutes each to present work.

So if it's a film we watch it or if it's a sculpture or painting we look at that and then discuss. We have had students really test out the parameters of the session as well. We had one performance artist who for his crit, *seminar,* got his friends to come in and beat him up in front of the group of students. It was quite scary really because I don't think anyone really knew what was going on until afterwards.

So they really beat him up?
Well it was staged but no one in the audience knew that. What with the health and safety culture that now pervades art schools, the increase in numbers, the erosion of studio space, it's really important that amongst all of that boring control stuff, unexpected things happen.

The decline in studio spaces is an economic thing…
It is. Space is increasingly expensive. Also, the art school here about five or six years ago was in a position where it had to expand its courses.

Why?
Because there wasn't a postgraduate or fine art research culture and a new Dean came in who really understood the importance of an art education within the context of other creative subjects.

What do you mean?
If you want really good fashion, graphics or interior design courses, it's good to have the art students there too, because they can be the most experimental. Having all of our students in the workshops doing stuff alongside all the other disciplines means that there's an exchange taking place.

Is it good for the reverse? Do art students benefit from mixing with those from other arts subjects?
Not always and that's a big drawback as we're finding out now. If its not a two-way exchange it makes me defensive actually.

A lot of people who come here aren't here because their parents wanted them to do it; they've had to battle with their parents to get here. There's a danger that in a larger institutional context it just becomes an add-on for all these other subjects that then get all the resources.

Does the college have a widening participation scheme and do you think it is an advantage if a student, influenced by their parents, has grown up to see contemporary art? Which type of student do you have most of here?
I think that the relative advantage changes as students move through the course. At times having knowledge of the subject can be useful and at other times it can be limiting.

Here, and I can only really talk about *here*, we interview a lot of students and our students come from a really wide range of backgrounds. We get a lot of students who come from Wales, Middlesbrough, Leeds and we also get some local people. What we're looking for I suppose is a commitment to the subject rather than a large knowledge necessarily. When students come in for their interview, what we're often looking for is this thing tucked away at the back of their portfolio, the thing that no one's really told them to do; it's something that they've done and they're not sure about, but we all want to find out more. It doesn't bother us what the students know about the subject at that point, it's just, are they committed? Do they have a unique view of the world? And will they survive what we're going to put them through and what they're going to put themselves through with us?

You've got to be immersed in the subject to do well. You've got to go to all the exhibitions and private views, read the books and be in the studio making work. Whether that's to do with social standing I'm not sure. I think problems occur when students aren't motivated to go and see things at all. That perhaps matters more than if their parents took them to see art or not.

We have a widening participation agenda at this university and that feeds down to all our courses.

Do you think that the skill of 'reading' art is something that can be just picked up through association with other people in crits or seminars?
I think it can. Say in a first year seminar someone comes in with three or four paintings. They'll talk about them and we'll ask a question like, "If you had to take away three of those paintings and just have one, which one would it be?" It's likely that they'll take away the three weaker ones and leave the one that is stronger. Then, for whatever reasons, if you ask the students in the seminar what they would have done, very often they'd make the same decision and we'd all be leaning the same way.

So you mean it's an intuitive skill?
I think it can be. I know that's probably not a very useful answer but there is a kind of visual sense, a heightened visual awareness that artists have. So for example, they understand the world through that stack of chairs over there …

(Points)

… Or that table or filing cabinet. They're looking and understanding what those things might mean visually.

You spoke about the importance of going to private views.
Yes.

Why do you think it is so important? Is it important that students go to see a lot of contemporary art?
I think it is important in order to create reference points so we can relate and compare work to other work in the field. It's not much different to a scientist developing a vaccine, by that I mean they'd have to be aware of other vaccines developed. Also, it's immersing yourself in the subject. You need to see as much work as you can, not because you'll like it all, but because occasionally you might see things that change the way that you think about your own work.

Do you think the work influences students at all?
I hope so. Not in the, "I'm going to copy or emulate that," kind of way, but more, "That's not the artist I want to be." I think it does influence. I think it should. Students aren't always influenced by the biggest, most sensational or outrageous artist but by a range of different things.

Skipping back a bit to when we were talking about the teaching of craft skills, do you think that the widespread decline in this sort of teaching is economic or pedagogic?
I don't know about other places but for us it's pedagogic. Certainly from my experience there was no real benefit in sticking to discipline-specific forms of art practice. Departmentalising subjects just used to set things in

opposition to each other, especially as resources got less. Artists often now work in quite diverse or broadly collaborative ways and so I think it helps pedagogically if you can release students from the idea that they're either a painter, sculptor, printer or film-maker etc in order that they can just see themselves as an artist making work in these different areas of practice. That can be a better situation to be in creatively. I wouldn't want to get to the end of my life and think, "Shit, I always painted but what I really wanted to do was stack bricks."

Do you think pedagogic approaches change in accordance with the times?
Perhaps. If you look at installation art, that was a term that was around when I was at college but now people don't really use it. But installation art still exists. Video art was a major thing and now it's just an integral part of practice.

Are you asking me if things will go back to being discipline specific?

I didn't, but it's an interesting question so please go for it ...
I think that once you let something out of a box it doesn't stop running and so I don't think it will ever go back. There is more accessibility for students to new processes and technologies now. When I wanted to work with film as a student I had to go and buy a reel of Super 8 film, send it off, wait three months, get the film back, set everything up work out some crazy looping device before I could show it. Nowadays you can make that same three-minute film in three minutes on your mobile phone or on a digital camera.

What is interesting to observe now though is that the aesthetics of those older formats are coming back. A lot of students now are doing woodcuts and linocuts but using it to make posters that they fly-post around town. Woodcutting is a very ancient process yet it is being used in a very modern way. In the same way, Super 8 is being used a lot in favour of modern technology.

Why do you think this is?
Maybe everything went so far the other way that now students are questioning whether the technological revolution delivered better art. Some are returning to old methods and techniques. Now if you see a woodcut image about town it stands out because its different and you think, "Well that's interesting, how did that get there?"

When you personally are looking at work both here and in gallery spaces, are there different criteria that you apply when evaluating the work you are looking at?
I think if I saw a brilliant piece of work made by a student I would have the same responses as if I saw a brilliant piece of work in the best gallery in London or New York, or Berlin. I'd still say, "That's a bloody good piece of art," and apply the same readings to both. The difference is that I am immersed here in the whole process of how that work came to be so the way I assess it is informed by knowledge I have from having spoken to that student in tutorials, having seen how they talk about that work in a seminar, having seen how they'd made decisions about how they use the space in terms of an exhibition and so on. It's a kind of privileged information.

Students know that we have a sliding scale of assessment that moves up through the levels of the degree course. So in the first year we are assessing things like studentship, attendance, participation in seminars and workshops signed up for. These all have a much higher weighting than the thing produced at the end. However, as students move through the course it becomes much more about the thing at the end and we take studentship as a given. Here we're assessing a student's progress throughout these stages of development and this is very different to assessing work in a gallery.

What 'goes on' in your evaluation of a gallery piece?
I suppose it depends on the artist. Let's take Mike Nelson's *Coral Reef* at the Tate as an example. I first saw that piece of work at Matt's Gallery in 2000 and felt that it transported me as a member of the audience into this other

kind of space. Art usually finds that very hard to do, even theatre finds that very hard to do, yet it created an atmosphere that was very profound and effecting on me and changed the way I see the world. And that I suppose is what really good art can do. Students' work can sometimes do that to me too.

So it's not like an MOT whereby you approach a piece of work, and say, "Passed on brakes, failed on windscreen wipers." It's much more complicated than that and I can appreciate why that's very hard for students to understand. But we actually have very clear assessment guidelines and this rolling scale of studentship. I'll give you the handbook, it's all in there.

Are you ever intimidated when you go into a commercial gallery space, or do you ever find yourself thinking, "I'm struggling to access this piece"?
I was intimidated by a lot of the galleries when I left college and so that's why I set up Space Explorations. I don't feel like that now though as there are a lot more galleries around and I'm used to it. But often I go to shows and think, "I don't get that," or, "What is that about?"

(Both laugh)

It takes a while to feel relaxed about your own work and it takes even longer before you can feel comfortable commenting on what someone else's work is doing.

You found out from your last book *[12 Gallerists: 20 Questions]* that it's a business at its ugliest end. But at its most interesting end it's something worthwhile that people can benefit from and get a whole lot out of. I've always resisted the business end. At the Slade we had a very non-commercial stance on it all. We didn't want galleries, they weren't where we were putting our energies, and we wanted to find something new.

As a student I felt little personal connection with West End Galleries and little desire to be involved with them. I suppose that in order to survive and make sure you're part of something you believe in, the best thing to do is ...
... Set up your own gallery.

Or projects, yeah.
Certain galleries have a lot of power. I found that quite uncomfortable so setting up my own things and teaching felt like a better way to live I suppose.
    I guess this side ...

(Points to the list of interview questions I have in my hand)

... you could say is mostly run by people who got into the field for the reason most of us get into the field – for art education. Whereas the other side ...

(Points to '12 Gallerists: 20 Questions', which is on the table in front of us)

... are more engaged in the commercial potential of what art education can produce.
    Education is becoming another business. If students have to pay in excess of £7,000, everything changes.

What do you mean by that?
So for instance students start to look around their studio space and say, "It's costing me £50 a day to be here."

Why do you have a degree show?
Because every year the modules that the students take are about developing a studio practice and then showing that in the form of an exhibition.

It's also this idea that art doesn't exist without it being located somewhere – part of the process of art practice is to negotiate everything that that means.

Our show is curated and so it also provides an education in negotiating the placement of your work alongside other people's. There is also the production of a publication that documents that work and it is promoted in order to get an audience. These are all things that are relevant to artists. We treat it not so much as a degree show but as an exhibition. We don't actually even call it the degree show. We just call it the final show. Hopefully it won't be for a lot of people!

(Both laugh)

I think it's important because people need to celebrate their work and also it's the only way you get critical and physical distance from it. In a way this goes back to your question about seeing work in a gallery context and seeing students work. At that point there's a fair comparison and you can apply some of the same thinking to each of those situations.

I think the students learn a lot from doing the show and I think it's a real bonding experience as well.

Do you have personal professional development modules?
We do but that's imbedded in everything really. Students write statements and do CVs but it's more about bringing in good examples of professional practice. I think we're trying to expose the undergraduate students to all of the components of a professional artistic life. They might argue that's not true. It's funny, when you get the NSS comments back it's always either, "The tutors were never there," or, "This is the most brilliant thing that's ever happened to me and has the most brilliant staff." It's one of those subjects where you get out of it what you put in I think. We tell them that at the open day now.

JANE LEE

Jane Lee is the BA Fine Art course director at Central Saint Martins
College of Art and Design, part of University of the Arts London.
We met in her office in Charing Cross Road in early November 2010.
This interview took place one day after the first student march against
the coalition governments proposed tuition fee rise.

Can you outline your position and how long you've been teaching on this course for?
I'm the BA Fine Art course director and I've been teaching here since
11ᵗʰ April 2007.

What did you do before you taught here?
I taught in Kent at the University of the Creative Arts and before that at
Glasgow School of Art. Before that I was at Edinburgh University and before that I taught a little while at University College London. Before all of
those were several other things but they were to do with medieval studies
at the British Library.

Whilst studying I was also Tony Caro's archivist for a little while –
that's my only real Saint Martins link now that I think about it!

Did you study art yourself?
No I didn't. I was trained as a historian and then as an art historian.

Did you go through any formal teacher training?
No, not my generation.

What made you decide to teach?

I came into teaching sideways really, through museum education. I was doing a lot of curating and part-time exhibition organising and I began teaching at the same time as doing that. I taught regularly at the British Library in their seminar rooms and galleries and I think that influenced me a lot. I was pretty good at it – good in the sense that it didn't freak me out or give me anxiety attacks – and I seemed to get it done properly. It was a typical woman's career at the time, what with having a small child to look after.

Do you think that art can be taught?

I don't think any subject can be taught in a didactic way. I think that you can set up an environment in which people learn things and that environment includes you sharing with them what you know and what you're enthusiastic about yourself.

Bodies of knowledge get passed along in art schools as well as skills such as writing, critical thinking, reading, and technicians are demonstrators of technical knowledge and skills.

The practical stuff gets taught in a direct way whereas the rest, the broadest part of our subject, develops through continuous investigation by the student. When we recruit students for an undergraduate degree we're looking for people who already have a continuity of practice, continuity that we're not to break, but encourage.

How do you do that?

We creatively and constructively intervene in a student's practice.

OK.

Which is what they want us to do. If they didn't why would they turn up? Art education is essentially that intervention into someone's practice I think.

Do you think it's important that students come to art college with some prior understanding of contemporary art and art history?
I think it's important that they understand why they want to come here and by default that usually involves some kind of understanding of contemporary art. I also don't think that you can consider someone to have an understanding of contemporary art unless they have some idea of the histories of art. And I say histories because of course there are several in that they are always created and constructed.

Do you teach art history on the course?
No we don't and as a historian that sometimes makes me grind my teeth. Some art history does get learnt as we go along, though I think it's a struggle really for students who have had no art historical training to get to grips with some of the relevant texts, as they don't have the references.

But one always has that problem. It's the same when people who are trying to do medieval studies have never studied Latin.

Do you think a knowledge of art history is helpful when reading art or making work of your own?
I do think that a young artist, who has the National Gallery just down the street as our students do here, is lucky. Rembrandt is as equally present as Yinka Shonibare, whose work is in Trafalgar Square, in front of the National Gallery. What's important is that what is interesting about the Rembrandt is actually up to the artist. There might be one artist who is interested in the relationship between Rembrandt and Caravaggio but another might go to see the Rembrandt to work out how he managed to get that white mark on the surface.

Do you think that students who come to study here without ever having visited galleries or museums whilst growing up, are at any disadvantage compared to those in their peer group who have?

Yes I think they are at a disadvantage but disadvantage doesn't just come through not having seen work in museums. It's also a disadvantage not to speak another language, not to have been to concerts, not to hear live music and not to play an instrument. How many of those can you tick that you can do? I can't tick all of them, as I don't play any instrument. I'd love to but instead I have to rely on other people telling me what's going on in a concert. I can't tell a violin from a bassoon. That's a disadvantage and I feel it.

What forms of teaching do you have here?
There is a mix of models that we use during the three years of the BA. We are currently moving from what I'd call fundamentally a tutorial model to Event Teaching, which is more focussed on specific types of processes, problems or ideas within the studio.

Can you unpack this a bit?
So, rather than someone turning up to give students a 15 minute tutorial, students instead have the chance to choose various kinds of events that they want to participate in, which they can then reflect on later. That gives us the chance to group the technical, critical studies, tutor, student and academic populations together into a particular event that may last two days or even a week. It may have 20-30 people participating or it may have fewer. Very often the events cut across pathways whereby one pathway will host a teaching event and invite people from other pathways to fill a certain number of places.

You run, is it four pathways within fine art? Can you say a bit about what they are and why you have pathways as opposed to just a broad fine art course?
We do have four pathways, yes. One reason I think for this is that it is such a large course. There are 556 students on the course!

Really?

Yes, and it's really key I think that people feel, as in any large community, that they have an address. So when we're recruiting people we look to see what their starting point is: what questions they're asking and what kind of conversations, as artists, they would best participate in. That will give them their pathway address.

For example, I recently recruited with Alex Ramsey [tutor at Central Saint Martins] who is great at spotting this. When he's looking through people's drawings it's exciting because he can, say, see that although a person whose work we are looking at has only ever worked in 2D, he can see the potential for sculpture in their drawings. The incoming student might not have had the facility to do sculpture in another place and so Alex would give them a 3D address right away so that they can talk about space, mass, scale and that sort of thing. Pathways are not exclusive material enclaves. Anyone in any pathway can work in any medium and has equal access to all technical resources.

Can you tell me a bit about your workshops? Does the course provide any level of technical instruction and do you think that such provision is an important or redundant part of art education now?

When people talk about workshops they might mean either a workshop's physical location – like underground where the wood workshop is – or they might mean a process-led sort of thing, where instruction goes on. What I'm trying to do is to move the process part with the technicians and demonstrators, out of those location workshops and into the studios to work alongside the students and tutors whenever that is possible. So what would happen for instance, would be that Caroline List, who runs workshops in the painting and supports workshop down in the cellar, would come into the painting studios with all of her kit and work with Mick Finch and his team in 2D. In the 2D pathway area they're really interested in different surfaces and repositioning different images on or against different surfaces and so it works really well. Technicians will sometimes suggest skills workshops in their areas to me and I'll support them if the budget meets it. I'll go around the studios and look at student work with technicians to make sense of the workshop they are proposing in terms of student practice.

With Event Teaching I'm trying to bring all of those moments together where everyone's there so every part of our teaching is present for the student in that event.

That sounds incredible.
So I don't know about other courses but we've increased our skills provision and we do have a thing about skills in the widest sense. Last year we brought in new technology called the International Display Initiative, which is LED (Light Electronic Diode) screens, computers and link computers. We have a specialist professor who oversees all of this and I had the first years inducted. I don't know much about it, though it is something that the University has a lot of faith in and something the students really enjoy, particularly those in 4D. Not only that, it has pushed forward the place of the distribution of the image to the top of the students' priorities.

Over the last couple of years I've also made sure that a lot of the staff development budget goes on sending academic staff out to learn new technical skills. For instance, someone might go and learn how to do Intaglio Printmaking, just so that we have someone in our team who knows these things. The technicians and all of us work very closely as a team.

There are also times in the course where students do a skills audit.

What's that?
It's where students realise what their current skills are and what skill they need to develop next. An opportunity to bump that skill up is then worked out. We are adding things like writing skills and learning a language before students go on Erasmus to the audit as well.

So there's a lot of provision.
Yes, but at the same time students must also know how to source additional things for themselves. It's no good people wanting to do things and not being able to because they don't have a technician to turn around to. They won't have one when they leave!

Can you talk a bit about the relationship between Central Saint Martins and Byam Shaw?
Yes, we are re-developing our relationship and we are now one course.

Some years ago, as with what happened in other small art schools, Byam Shaw was on the point of bankruptcy and needed to be made part of a bigger institution. It joined with Central Saint Martins and as a result of that the University and the College had to look for ways in which all of their constituent parts could best run together. There are guidelines given to us by HEFCE who give us our government money and want to see that we're doing everything efficiently. They couldn't see why there were two courses, which to them were exactly the same only one big and one small, running with two separate operating costs.

It made sense from an academic point of view to have one large course and be able to provide a variety and depth of education. It came to the point when we had to re-validate our courses – all courses get revalidated every few years – and we worked together to become one large BA Fine Art course. This model is also now in a sense being used on our Masters degree level as well.

Thanks in great part to Joanna Greenhill, who has recently retired as its director; Central Saint Martins School of Art has had a very successful MA Fine Art for many years. Byam Shaw also had both an MA and a postgraduate diploma course in fine art, each with their own traditions. We were all eager to build new postgraduate provision and so all of the graduate teaching teams and colleagues from other fine art courses within CSM, brought together their ideas and energy and we now have three MAs. There is an MA in Fine Art, an MA in Photography, and an MA in

Art and Science. We also have an MRes (Master of Research), which has three pathways: Exhibition Studies, lead by the team that publishes the journal of exhibition studies *Afterall;* Moving Image, in partnership with *Lux*; and Philosophy and Theory. We had a really radical look at everything and in a way, have started again.

Will the Byam Shaw space at Elthorne Road remain?
Yes. Both of the Byam Shaw buildings will be retained and used largely for fine art. The MA studios will be there, as will our first year studios. There is a lot of development happening there with regards to our skills priorities for the course. We're developing the sculpture area a little, the whole of the first floor of the main building will be a printmaking area to be used by the whole College, and what used to be the library is already now a reading room where we already have two members of staff leading art-writing projects. We hope to make it a centre of practice that will work with specialist organisations such as Bookworks and attract the attention of small publishers.

It is important that we retain all of the good things that came into the mix when we brought our courses together. Attention to making is one of the things that the Byam Shaw team felt was part of their tradition and in continuing that we are also perhaps reviving that tradition from the Central School as well. This is not the first time we have been involved in combinations.

Combining things always has its critics of course but we are already seeing the advantages. When we are at Kings Cross the fact that we will have brought all of our libraries together from across the college will give us an amazing new resource.

Can you talk a bit about Central Saint Martin's impending move to Kings Cross?
From next academic year, the CSM fine art programme courses will be housed both at Kings Cross and Byam Shaw. First Year students will have

their studios at Byam Shaw but will have some of their workshops and all of their lectures and seminars at Kings Cross. They may well find themselves at Kings Cross for various event teaching and optional projects as well. Second and third year studios will be at Kings Cross as will their seminar and lecture programmes. They will go to the Byam Shaw campus for some specialist workshops, particularly for all forms of printmaking and for book arts. Some off-site events and projects involve the Archway area and second year students might find themselves using Byam Shaw campus as a base for those whenever it is required. The library for everyone will be at Kings Cross. Kings Cross also has a full working theatre and other advantages that will be part of the whole College's experience. As I haven't yet seen it with the roof on – we all still have to be inducted into the building – it is difficult to go into a great deal of detail. The MAs, MRes and PhD students will have a large base room and teaching facilities and workshops at Kings Cross but will have their studios at the Byam Shaw campus. We have a few projects in the area and our students are already scoping out their new neighbourhood. We have a lot of research links with France and Belgium and being near the Eurostar terminus is a plus for us. I'm also looking forward to being so close to the British Library.

I'm a bit worried about saying too much about what we're going to do because, especially being an art school, people don't like it if they think you've got more space than they have – and we haven't!

(Both laugh)

Did you hear me say 556 students on one course alone?

Secondly, take a look at my ceiling!

(Points above our heads to a ceiling with holes and parts of the plaster falling away)

I could take you into the next room where the water falls freely ...

So it's purely structural, the reason you are moving?
Yes. These buildings are too hard to keep up and we can't plough all of our money into keeping up really run-down old buildings when the costs are going up everywhere and there's little money to support students. We have an awful lot of work to do just to keep the studios warm enough for people not to die in them in the winter! We have to do the most efficient thing.

What's the general mood like regarding the move?
Everybody loves the current Charing Cross Road school and it's such a romantic thing I guess being in the middle of Soho. But the reality is that a bit of my heritage falls on my desk every Monday morning.

We are archiving the buildings and gathering together everything we can find which illuminates its history and the histories of those who used it. Students have also been working with staff to uncover the changing pedagogies of Central Saint Martins.

A couple of months ago Central Saint Martins hosted a conversation with Peter Kardia about 'The Locked Room.'

Yes I remember reading about it. That came after a whole spate of conversations on art education. What are your thoughts on the perceived current 'crisis' in art education?
I know the students and also Dan Mitchell, an associate lecturer on the Foundation course at Backhill who wrote to the journal. What Dan was speaking about had nothing to do with this course and there was a lot of misinformation. A lot of people have a fantasy about what's going on and then respond to that.

A lot of people have been saying that art education, post-Thatcher and after polytechnics became universities, has lost something in the transition. Do you think this is true in any way?

Of course it has lost something since then. However, I think our dean made the point that in Peter Kardia's day, six per cent of people went into higher education and now nearly 40 per cent do. Of course there's an awful lot lost when you're not living in an entirely elitist, over fêted society and when you've done your 'widening participation'. If that generation want to turn around and say, "Well, it should be the way it was when we were more privileged," I think it's likely that some people will say, "Yes, it damn well should, it should be as it was for you for everybody." However, I would remind them that we thought they were the ones who were fighting for the *end* of privilege!

Funding to higher education has increased but it has nowhere near kept pace with widening participation. When there are more of you and there is less of everything it does not necessarily mean a 'crisis'. It does however, demand that everyone is effective, dedicated and respectful of others enough to benefit from the different riches we bring each other.

So do you think that the points being made are a result of generational nostalgia?
Yes. What's also worth mentioning though is that whereas many of my colleagues my age – I'm sixty – went through the art school system, I went through the university system and so I'm not as much of a stranger to it.

But I think even back then the art schools were getting closer to the university system than they realised. I think the Coldstream report and the closure of small art schools brought the big art schools in London closer to the university population. So did other things like May '68 in Paris, which made all students think differently about the political and social position of the student.

Nevertheless it was and is a big change. It's very difficult to be plonked into the university and to have to alter the way you are used to doing things. It's not just art schools that had to do this though, lots of medical schools had to do the same thing. In my generation, doctors would be educated in St Thomas' in the hospital where they did on-site medical training. Now that training has to be done within the university and to be a doctor you have to have a university education. People are going to say,

"That's not the right way to train a doctor," or, "That's not the right way to train an artist." I don't say either is and or isn't the right way. UAL is lucky in that it is a specialist university that formed itself. In many ways it is much harder for 'faculties' of fine art in general universities.

Many people who complain about the end of a tradition are reacting to the increase in audit mechanisms that came in during the Thatcher years and caused a great deal of unproductive bureaucracy to grow in universities. This is wasting away now and we are beginning to feel the benefit of that change.

There are clearly different opinions about the best way to deliver a fine art course...
Yes and to give a further example, we have a really good Erasmus and exchange programme here. I have to fit students from this course into other courses abroad which are very different to ours and vice-versa. I know someone who works at an art school in New York, and they have a completely different university system whereby everyone is engaged in a class at every moment and seemingly students never get into the studio! On the other hand, in Berlin, our Erasmus colleagues seem not to have any academic structure at all of any kind! You're lucky if they have an academic programme that doesn't rely on the whim of the Meister der Kunst. I'm polarising of course but you get my point.

How long is an Erasmus exchange for?
Three months normally but it can be extended to finish a semester in another system.

In terms of when you personally are assessing work in either a contemporary gallery or in a studio here, what is the process going on inside your head as you are looking at the work? What evaluative criteria are you using?

In the University there is a list of very particular criteria and those on the team, for it is never just one person assessing work, are all quite clear with each other about what they mean by these different criteria and how they would find them in a work. They walk around and do what you call a 'parity' exercise, which means that they tell each other, "I find these criteria in this work," or, "I find this in this work," until they know that they're all on the same wavelength. They then mark against those criteria and check again. Within the art school there's no, "I like this work," or, "I don't like this work," it doesn't work like that at all. It's a very serious and complex thing and even though I don't think it necessarily takes this PG Cert training-to-be-teachers thing, it does take mentoring and a real sense of responsibility. Those two situations you just described, the gallery and the students' work, are never confused.

Though I do find it difficult sometimes to go into a gallery and not say, "That's a good 2:1!"

(Both laugh)

In a way, teaching in an art school teaches you to become much better at accepting things that you don't know about. I occasionally go into quite young galleries and see things that I do kind of step back from. I put them into a research capsule in order to try and better understand the work.

Why do you have a degree show?
Largely, I have to admit it's because there was one when I came. Also, I haven't seen any reason not to. It is, as on most courses, a unitised framework. We could examine without it but we're giving people the privilege of having a show in the West End.

Does it form part of a student's professional development?
The marketing department does all of the invitations and the students raise

money for a catalogue. There's also a company called Artscom, which are the part of the University that run our short course and manage our study abroad programmes, who come in to help with the sales and help students with the pricing of their work. They work very effectively with the students. They handle sales of work on the night and I also do a lot of selling. Marketing brings in collectors and the Dean and I take people around. We usually sell about £35,000-£40,000 worth.

Really?
Oh yes, and that is one of the reasons for keeping the degree show because some students actually pay off a chunk of their debt by selling at the show.

Wow.

The debt levels look set to get worse; the fees are about to go up astronomically, perhaps as high as £9,000.
Yes, we haven't been told what ours will be yet. Obviously there's a way out of charging these. The government could stop the war in Afghanistan, stop bombing Iraq, scrap Trident and give all of that money to students. But until that happens this is what we have to work with and we do our best.

Do you think that students come to art school now expecting a career at the end?
I don't know. I see a lot of students who come to open days and a lot of them have rather broad and grandiose ideas about what can be done with their degree. As the number of well-educated people in Britain rises, having degree level education is seen as the norm. People now are more aware that a degree doesn't necessarily guarantee you a job or any terrific advantage in the labour market. Instead I think they realise that you do a degree for all of the human reasons and that you want to go on learning. A fine

art degree is a really good degree for that, and for learning the key skills of being able to teach yourself.

So it's a choice of life. It's, "I want to be this kind of person," a person who has this exciting interior life that connects them to the rest of society in a particular way. Essentially, I would say that most of the students come with that as their priority, rather than a career. Artists are versatile and multi-skilled and many are fairly good entrepreneurs in their own right. Art education establishes and improves this and art school educated people are more likely than others to be able to think of a new industry from the ground up. When governments recognise the value of 'creativity' this is what they are valuing.

Of course students don't want to be hobbled in making a living when they leave and so we try to make that easier for them.

How?
We've brought in a new fourth year.

What's that?
It's a Professional Practice Diploma that the student can elect to take between second and third year. In a way it's an internship, whereby students go out for twenty weeks of placements supervised by the college. That earns students an extra 120 credits – good for European placements on top of a degree, such as that at the Jan Van Eyck Academy. Students also get a connection to the industry and an opportunity to make a lot of contacts.

The people supporting that diploma are very experienced in making that happen. Many people do an internship and then go back there for a first job. So in a sense that shifts the degree vocationally for those who do it. But within the other three years there are also times where transferable skills are developed. We have offsite projects in second year that help people learn how to work in the world.

Do people find the placements themselves?
They do but the college has a lot of contacts and this helps them with a lot of opportunities being offered. Central Saint Martins enjoys a lot of professional good will.

MICHAEL ARCHER

Michael Archer is programme leader for the BA Fine Art course at Goldsmiths College, part of the University of London. He is also a well known critic and writer on art. We met in his office on the 10ᵗʰ November 2010, the day of one of the first student marches against the coalition government's proposed tuition fee increase.

Please could you outline what your position is and how long you've been teaching on this course for?
I am the programme leader for the BA Fine Art course and I've been working here for just over a year now.

What did you do before you came to Goldsmiths?
Before I came here I was the head of department at the Ruskin School of Drawing and Fine Art at Oxford University. Before that I was a senior lecturer at Chelsea and before that I was also teaching here at Goldsmiths part-time on the BA Fine Art course as a critical studies tutor. And before that I was teaching at Wimbledon.

Was it always the Critical Studies side you taught on?
Not entirely. When I first started I was doing studio teaching. I started doing Critical Studies at one point because somebody was ill and I got asked to do a lecture as there wasn't anybody else to do it. And I carried on from there.

Did you study art yourself?
No I didn't. I went to university to study Natural Sciences. I did two years of natural sciences – which included physiology, pharmacology, experimental psychology and biochemistry – and then I changed subject and did one year of Art History.

That was to say, I was always interested in art.

Did you grow up looking at art?
Up to a point. I mean I did look at art for sure and my father taught woodwork, metalwork and ceramics in a teacher-training college. A lot of the things we had in the house were made by him; so the chairs we sat on, the table we ate off, the bowls we ate out of – they were all made by my father. He had a workshop and so I saw him in there a lot – and that was really I think the way I got into understanding how the eye, the hand and the mind can work together in the presence of materials. And obviously there were loads of books around about art and I started to look at art and think, "I like this."

But by that time I was doing science A-levels and they seemed kind of easy so I ended up doing science at university. But as I say, I knew that I was interested in art so I changed.

How and when did your writing career begin?
Not straight away. The first place I worked after university was the Whitechapel Gallery, installing the shows and then invigilating when the shows were up. That was quite a long time ago and at a time when far fewer people came to the gallery than they do now.

Like most galleries we sold magazines. I couldn't afford to buy any and so I just read them whilst I was invigilating. After a bit I guess I just thought, "I could do that." So I wrote something and sent it to a magazine and they said OK.

So what then made you decide to teach?
One of the people who I met when I worked at the Whitechapel was Bill Furlong. Bill had just started Audio Arts, which was a magazine published on audiocassette. In addition to doing several issues already, he commissioned a couple of works on tape-slide – something that was, at that time, an extraordinarily wonderful new medium.

These works were shown at the Whitechapel and so I worked with him on the show. I was already thinking by that time that I might be writing criticism and so I was interested in the kind of spaces in which critical practice could be developed. The space of the audiotape seemed very interesting and Audio Arts – which for Bill was in a very large and very obvious way his art practice – was also something that engaged in a kind of critical examination of what other art practices there were around. That seemed to be a very rich area to get involved in and so I worked with Bill for over a decade as Audio Arts.

So because I was doing that, because by that time I was doing some commissions in the education department at the Whitechapel, and because I was kind of au fait with using sound and image, I was just asked to go and do some teaching on those kinds of projects in art schools. And so I started teaching.

Do you think art is a subject that can be taught?
I think it is a subject that you can't instruct people on. I also think that the word 'teach' is quite a large one. Maybe if we go back to the meaning of words: if we think of education rather than teaching or instruction, education might be a better word to use. This is really obvious, but if we think of the literal meaning of the word 'educate' – which means 'to lead out of ...', then I think that's what being at an art school might be more about. It's a process of allowing what is already there in the students to find a way out. The major part of what you're doing as a tutor is not ramming stuff in but actually discussing openly what the students are interested in, what they're engaged or involved in and having a constructive conversation about that.

It's having a conversation that is reflective and critical and that opens up or investigates ways in which stuff can be expanded upon, deepened or progressed.

So it leans towards a kind of 'self-discovery'?
I think that's certainly the case. What I find very rich about it is that whilst there are many instances where you are with groups of students and are engaged in quite a complex interchange, in an important sense a lot of it is one to one. That is to say, it's about what each of the individual students are doing rather than the notion of teaching that says, "I have you all in a room, now let's all learn how to do this." That won't get you very far.

I just graduated from this course and so unlike the other interviews I did, I have direct experience of the course I am asking questions about. I want to ask:

There is a contemporary art lecture series here, which is great for provoking lots of thought and questions. However, because I did a year of Art History before studying on this course, I think when I first joined I was thinking, "Where is the art history?" I wondered how we were supposed to place our work and ideas, or draw references without any taught knowledge of it. What are your thoughts on this? Is there a reason for not teaching art history on the course?
I think we have to make a distinction between whether art history should be taught and whether there is anything of interest, use or value in what has happened in art before now. Clearly a lot of what has happened in art before now may well be extraordinarily useful or of interest to different students engaged in different things. But that's not the same as saying, "Everybody ought to be taught art history." I think that if the structure of the course is such that art history is an implicit part of it, it's quite easy to allow students to gain the impression – however strenuously you deny this – that there is this thing called art that has a history: this person did something, then this person did something and then this person did something else.

And we have a number of famous examples from over the years until eventually we get up to now – the present day.

So we have this huge pile of extraordinary achievements that students are being shown and then we say to them, "So here you are, now go and do it," which is to say, "Everything you have to do must at least match everything that we just told you. Before you even start we're going to shackle you, we're going to weigh you down, we're going to put a big ball and chain on your leg and we're going to restrict your imagination, your curiosities, your whims, your quirks, your fancies, your experimentations – all of those things. And we're going to make sure you don't do all these things because we're telling you that everything you do has to be as good as Michelangelo." That's really not a sensible way to proceed.

That's not to say, by the way, that Michelangelo is not wonderful; I'm absolutely not saying that. I'm also not saying that lots of students don't get an awful lot from looking at it. But in terms of the way in which it's understood that students might access it and start to assimilate what it has to offer, we have to be careful of that.

I totally understand what you just said, and I think it's fascinating. I was just wondering however, if in your opinion it helps if people come to the course with a vague understanding of art history? Or do you think it's irrelevant?
I think probably I'd say that knowing something of the history of art might well be entirely to someone's benefit. But I also would not want to say that that should be prioritised over having knowledge of other things.

And I suppose art is a subject where you can bring in references from all over the place?
Yes. I think one of the things that the inclination to demand a thorough knowledge of art history relates to is the idea that art practice is containable within a certain set of skills – that there are things one needs to be able to do in order to be an artist.

Such as…?

Such as, you need to be able to paint or you need to be able to know what a painting is and how to make one. That you need to be able to do a life drawing and to be able to pick up a chisel and do something. That you need to be able to do certain things with a piece of wood, or be able to get an image, make a screen of it and put that image onto a piece of paper. Those sorts of things are very understood ways in which artists have operated for some time. And along with, "We need to teach you the history of art," goes, "We need to teach you these things and once we've taught you both of those things then we've taught you to be an artist." Or we've at least taught you what being an artist might require you to do.

But being an artist may encompass so much now that this narrowly defined set of skills can't possibly be enough.

So is that the reason for most art schools no longer teaching craft-based skills and technical instruction? Although the workshops are there, few people 'teach' them as such…

Well again, I think that to think of that as being some kind of loss would be to say that a narrowly-defined set of specific craft skills are just the ones you need in order to do art or to be an artist. But it might not be those skills you need to do the things you are doing. There might be other types of skills; certain discernments, certain ways in which you search material out, how you make choices about it, how you select it, how you put one thing next to another. Maybe putting one thing next to another involves the ability to weld. It might also involve other kinds of facilities which are digital.

So how should people go about acquiring the particular skills they need – should they just go out and get them themselves?

There are two ways. One is that a large number of skills can be learnt via the technicians. What we do here is offer a range of spaces where technicians who are very familiar with the skills, work. They can teach the students what they might need to know and that's done on a 'need to know' basis. If what you're doing means that you need to know how to use a tufting gun because you need to make a rug then you go and find out how to do that. But not everyone needs to know how to make a rug so we don't teach everyone how to do that.

So that's one way. The other way is that as part of the learning experience, there should be the development of a real sense that one needs to be proactive. So if you recognise that there is a need to do something then indeed part of being an artist is that you go out and find where and how that need can be met. In the jargon that's called Personal and Professional Development.

I had a question about whether the decline in technical instruction came about as a political or pedagogic choice or if it was merely a result of economics...
I do not believe that there has been a decline in technical instruction. There are all kinds of things that we understand historically to be involved in the making of these things we understand as works of art.

An analogy might be to say that if today I'm faced with the task of getting from here to Newcastle, I don't get on a horse.

(Both laugh)

I don't ride a horse from here to Newcastle or get in a horse-drawn carriage from here to Newcastle. I get on a train. I get on a train because there is a train. Now of course, I could if I wanted to, get on a horse from here to Newcastle, but that would be a very particular thing to do and most people don't do that. So there's a certain aspect of this insistence or this nostalgia for particular ways of working that connects with that. It's, "I think people should still be getting on their horse."

The course here is not divided by medium, by painting or sculpture pathways. It's just called Art Practice – or now Fine Art. I believe Goldsmiths was one of, if not the first place to do this. Do you know how and why this decision came about?
Firstly I don't feel confident in saying it was the absolute first. The best thing to do would be to read what Jon Thompson [head of Goldsmiths art department in the eighties] has written about art education.

I think at the root of it is that the organisation of an art school into clearly defined category areas such as the painting studio, the sculpture studio, and, in the late sixties and early seventies, the 'other place' for time-based or mixed media, suggests that there is something almost prior to the activity of art making that needs to be taken into consideration. There's almost a sort of censorship.

What I mean is that if what you do is paint, then you can carry on painting and that's never at issue. But the idea that somehow because you walk through a certain door or you work on a certain floor in a building, that what you are doing is therefore painting, is restrictive. What increasingly became important was that you should think first of all about whether you are making this thing as a painting that might actually want to be something else, something for its own sake, for its own sense of itself. So instead it became, "OK, everyone here is making art," and that seemed to open things up much more.

And you agree with that way of structuring things ...?
I do agree, yes.

There's a long-standing myth or rumour that circulates amongst both prospective and current students – at any art college – that Goldsmiths is 'The conceptual place'. The perception is that Goldsmiths favours 'making through thinking', rather than 'thinking through making'. I also mentioned this to John Aiken, as the Slade tends to be typecast as the reverse. What do you think about this? Is it all merely a rumour or do you believe there to be any weight to it?

I can see why from the outside people might think that that's not what goes on here but I highly disagree with that. I want to refute it for sure.

Clearly it's a very discursive space here, people are talking all of the time. But they're absolutely doing it whilst they're making, through their making, and in relation to their making.

Can I ask you about the convenor?
Of course.

The convenor is a Goldsmiths model whereby six or seven students have about 25 minutes each for the presentation and discussion of work. I wondered if you could say a bit about its distinctiveness and what sets it apart from the regular art school 'crit'?
Well the group crit is not unique to Goldsmiths and in a sense that's all we're saying – that it's a group crit. Though I suppose to give it more of a face in terms of this school, it involves the presence of more students than are showing – which might not always be the case elsewhere. So there is a much broader conversation and there are many more potential angles through which something can be discussed.

I don't think it's unique to the convenor that one would not only ever be talking about finished work, because that is also the case in other crit situations, when you're presenting the beginning of something or an idea you're working on but have not yet resolved. In those cases the conversation is part of the process of resolution.

What is important about it for me I think is the degree to which the students' voices are predominant. There are only ever two tutors present in the convenors here. It's not that any tutor can just drop-in and it's certainly always the case that the discussion and debate that is developed around and through the presentation of work is initiated and led by the student and not the tutors. It's never the point of the tutor's presence to say what's right or wrong, good or bad. They can and do contribute, but they're not in charge.

The other thing of course is that the students are from all three years. That's key. So it's not just a group of, say, second years talking to themselves. We're never in a space in which everyone understands that they are all at the same stage of anything. There is a cross talk from the first years to the third years and back again.

Someone who is new onto the course might present something and the discussion might allow them to realise that in fact there are all kinds of areas where things need to be developed. Then someone who is later on in the course might present something and the conversation from newer voices might allow them to see that they've started to make assumptions about things in their work that they really shouldn't have started to make assumptions about.

In a convenor everyone looks at and discusses the work. Is that the place where the skill of learning to 'read' art and think about art is acquired, or develops?
It's one of the places, because people are looking at what's being presented and making comments about it. It becomes evident what people are looking at, how they are looking, what they are seeing, why they might be seeing the things they are seeing, why they might be focussing on things, why it is possible to focus on things, why the work is allowing or suggesting certain things to be focussed on. Also the questions about material, why certain materials work the way they do; all of those things are what happen in the convenor conversation. But it's not the only place. Those conversations also happen in the studios, in the workshops, in galleries …

Let's say that you personally are looking at a work in a gallery that you've never been to before. The work is by an artist whose work you've never seen before. It's not like here where you know the students and the context of their making. Can you, in this situation, look at that new work and make an instant value judgement or reading of the work? Or is it just, "I like that," and then you'd have to go away, research and think about the potential deeper context of the work?

I don't think that's ever what I do or ever what I have done. One of the things that really interests me about teaching, one of the things I like about it, is being in that position of 'not knowing'. As you say, I do know a lot of the students here and I kind of know what work they're doing. But at the same time I really relish the fact that when I go to a student's space and sit down I absolutely do not know what they are going to show me. I also know that it is going to be demanded of me that I engage in some sort of conversation about this. And I really like that.

In a way that's what I like about writing, too. It's the process of writing that allows the development of an idea or the articulation of some set of notions that can only come in relation to the experience of being with and looking at the art. The writing is not an explanation of the art and it's not a judgement on the art; it's something that comes out of the experiencing of the art. And the least interesting things one can say is, "this is good," or, "this is bad." Though you might in the end conclude that because it has stimulated you to write something that suggests that it's got something substantive about it.

Many of those who went to art school in the sixties have been speaking recently about the apparent difference in motive between students who went to art school in their generation and those who come now. They say that their generation went to art school because of some sort of 'calling' that they had. Students now are accused of seeing art as something that may lead to a glamorous career. This notion is amplified a hundred-fold when thinking about students studying at a place such as Goldsmiths, with its renowned alumni and the legacy of the YBA phenomenon. Do you think there is any truth in this?
I don't know. I think clearly the field of education is very different now to the way it was then. If you go back to that time, we're still only just getting to the point where it's even possible to do anything like get a degree by going to art school. That's also the period during which art schools that had been independent were becoming absorbed into larger higher education institutions.

The kinds of things that have happened in education go hand-in-hand with the sorts of things we see happening in art. We can talk about Conceptualism, we can talk about the way in which Biennales have grown up, the way in which the market has developed, and the way in which the prize culture has blossomed over the last 25 years. All of those things seem to be very intricately linked. I don't know about people saying, "I need to go to a particular art college in order to get a job." Everyone needs a job. It doesn't seem to be the over-riding concern that I sense amongst the students here.

Can you outline the philosophy of the course?
It's a difficult question because it's one that invites a sort of sound bite answer. It says, "Could you reach onto the shelf where you've got that, take it down and read it out to me?"

In a sense, what I would say is that I can just repeat everything I've just said to you. There are things we see – not just me but all of us teaching on this course – to be really quite significant elements in it. For one, the fact that it is a fine art course and that people from the moment they come in here are understood to be making art. It's understood that what we're doing when talking to them is recognising that they're making art at the stage they're making it and that their art needs to be addressed, discussed, drawn out and developed from that understanding, rather than being – to go back to the art history question – held up against something else and told, "It's not that, therefore it's inadequate."

Secondly, it comes out of a conversation with the students. Third, it takes place in an environment where all of the students are involved: first, second and third years. Physically it occurs in spaces in which students from all years are present and working. And it's everything we've just talked about. I do not have a three-sentence answer to your question. But I also think that it's perhaps important that there is no three-sentence answer. And I think if you ask any of the other tutors here they would go on about all of those things I've just mentioned, too.

ROSEMARIE McGOLDRICK

Rosemarie McGoldrick is the BA Fine Art course leader at Sir John Cass School of Art, part of London Metropolitan University. We met in her office on Tuesday 14th December, five days after the coalition government passed the decision – on recommendations made by the Lord Browne report – to raise the cap on tuition fees.

Can you tell me about your role here?
I am the course leader for BA Fine Art at Sir John Cass School of Art and my role is to make sure that the course runs well.

What does that entail?
I have to make sure that all of the modules work in the right way and that all of the information students and staff need is communicated. I am also responsible for recruiting hourly-paid staff on the course. My policy is to recruit a really good and varied group of practitioners who are well known and well shown: experienced tutors who are artists first, who show their work regularly, who are active researchers, who are good teachers and who each bring something very different to the students.

Saying this is making me think about my time at Chelsea where we never saw most of our tutors as they were always down the pub! There were equal numbers of staff to students but that didn't matter, as we never actually saw them. On the other hand, I did my MA at Goldsmiths and there we constantly had fantastic practitioners come in to talk. I may have had a three-hour tutorial – which is a long time – that could change the direction of my work, and that was exciting.

So my aim is to get as many good artists talking to students, talking about their work and showing their work really.

In one of your emails to me you asked if I could remember to always refer to the college as the Cass School.
Yes.

What is the importance of that?
Well the Cass has a long history and has always had references back to the City, where its patron Sir John Cass was from. The BA started out as a HND course and lots of people who hadn't got their A levels or O levels could come in, do printmaking once a week, and it was quite an accessible sort of course. It then went on to merge with City of London College to become the City of London Polytechnic, before being awarded university status and changing its name to London Guildhall University in 1992. In 2002 London Guildhall University merged with the University of North London to become London Metropolitan University – the largest university in London.

There is of course another reason. In 2009 London Met was fined heavily by HEFCE as a result of the University's confusion over student numbers and hence we're now £40 million in debt. This year the old department changed into a Faculty, with us going back to being a School of Art again, which is fantastic and means that whenever anyone refers to London Met being £40 million in debt – which has a very negative feel about it – our art students are able to instead identify with something that isn't negative: the Cass.

It's a bit like Slade, Goldsmiths or Chelsea. All of those colleges are part of a bigger institution but you don't say, "Chelsea, University of the Arts London," or, "Goldsmiths, University of London," every time do you? It's an important thing for us to be identified as an art school rather than some sort of huge university that's very difficult to get your mind around.

We've also got the Cass Business School in the city, which used to be connected with us and hopefully that relationship will start to blossom again.

Is the school supported financially by the Cass Foundation?
The Faculty is, in a small way, I think, though I'm not sure how. The Cass Foundation is a charity. I think it supports the University of East London (UEL) as well.

One thing that I am trying to do, particularly in these hard times, is to look out for businesses that might offer some sort of scholarships to students. The great thing about the Cass, which is I think different to most art colleges, is that our cohort of students is ethnically very mixed. We've got lots of Eastern European students, lots of students from down the road in Muslim areas, as well as white middle and working class students. It's not a finishing school. The college has always had a good reputation for bringing in students from other areas and representing well the area we are in. That gives the place a different energy and a different urge for learning I think. New lecturers here always comment on that.

We also get students who have never been to art galleries before as it's just not where they've come from. They come from a background of having never visited these places yet all of a sudden you see them just blossom! They gain confidence, and confidence in their work.

I don't think it has escaped anyone's notice that universities recently got the go ahead to put their fees up to as high as £9,000. What do you think of this? Will it change things? Will it alter the demographic Cass is proud to have studying here?
It can't *not* change things, really. It will affect most of the country's children and families. Art is four years of study, what with the Foundation and the BA, and if you haven't got the money you're going to think about it seriously! Students are going to come out with a huge amount of debt.

The government is not giving anything to the arts and that is just shocking. Arts feed society, they are just so important. To deny that is criminal. Patrick Brill, also known as Bob and Roberta Smith, is a member of the teaching staff at the Cass and he wrote a wonderful piece in The Guardian talking about how this is the worst thing that's happened to the arts since book burning and the Reformation of the Monasteries.

In the Times the other day – I don't usually buy the Times but it was the only newspaper there – was a cartoon of these two tramps on a park bench. One of them says, "I'm the first one in my family ever to go to university." It could be like that.

Did you get a grant to study?
Yes. I mean, it used to be delayed but that didn't matter because I could live off of my travel expenses. It is a *completely* different world now and I don't know what's going to happen, I really don't. I've spoken to people who aren't at university and have no intention of going and they don't agree with it either. I think that everyone feels that if they had kids they'd like them to go through higher education.

University is an incredible growing time. You meet people you'd never have met before, research and develop practice and develop relationships with people that stick once you leave university. It's just an important thing to be able to experience.

I don't know how all of this is going to change our relationship as tutors to our students.

How do you mean?
Well, I was talking to someone from New York the other day, trying to find out – what with the huge fees they pay over there – what the relationships are like there between staff and students. It's sounds like it's far more compromised over there, especially over grades. The worry is that we could get to a stage where students say, "Well actually, I don't like what you're teaching and I'm paying your wages, so therefore you should change it." We need a situation where we can teach our best form of art education without anything else getting in the way.

So you mean students will become and act like consumers?

Yes. But consumers of what, knowledge? The great thing about the University now is that as staff we say to students that we are critically tough in order to develop their practice and make them critically tough on themselves. We risk letting students down if we don't provide that. But the high fee paying student may not want to hear criticality and if they all begin to say so that will change everything.

Do you think that students enter art courses now with the expectation of a career at the end?

I think there is a sense of responsibility on students now. What you've done with Q-Art has been incredibly pro-active and you've gone out there, met people and allowed others to meet people. That's something that is important now more so than ever.

When I was at Chelsea it was fun but there was almost also a bit of impotence about it too. It wasn't, "Let's go out there and put on a show because we can," it was more, "Let's wait until a gallery picks us up." There were fewer galleries and everything was about waiting for somebody else to do it for you. Nowadays, especially since Goldsmiths and Freeze, there's a real kind of 'can do' attitude amongst students; they see that they can go and do things. There are a large number of students from Cass who now have their own gallery spaces or get exhibition spaces for a night down in Commercial Street. It's very different from when I was at Chelsea.

We now have a situation where we teach professional development to students too and we teach them how to apply for funding and things.

When did you go through art education?

I finished my BA at Chelsea in the early eighties and I finished my MA at Goldsmiths in 1990. I started a PhD at UEL in the early 1990s, right at the beginning when not many artists were doing PhDs, but I didn't finish. There wasn't the support for them then like there is now.

How long have you been teaching here?
Fifteen years. As course leader, though I'm just going into my second year now.

You mentioned in our last email that you are currently writing the new BA course, due to launch in 2012. Can you tell me a bit about this, if you can?
I can't really. I've definitely got some ideas about how I'd like it to be but it will all be organised through consultation with students, alumni, staff and various experts. It's not going to be just left until the last minute, so we just get a bodged version of the same old thing; that's too easily done. I'm sure it will focus more on professional practice and making a living in the art world.

Will it stay as a broad-based fine art course?
Yes.

OK.
Do you think that's a good thing or bad thing?

Me? I think …
I think most students prefer it this way. I remember when I was at Chelsea, the painters were upstairs and we were downstairs in sculpture and there was a real divide. Our classes were small – about twelve – and I remember someone in my sculpture class doing photography and someone said, "Oh, you can't do that here." It was very peculiar. It was, "they're the painters, they're the sculptors and they're the print makers." Oh, and I forgot the Graphic Design lot – they were the rich Sloane Ranger types!

(Both laugh)

So there was no real crossover, which was a real shame. In this day and age I like that I can see painters working with film, sculptors working with photography and so on. That that happens is a reflection of the layout and structure of the art school.

It's almost as if current course structures are the improvements that their leaders would have liked to have seen in their own education?
Maybe. It's important to hire teachers who are close to the students in age terms as they're the ones who help get over that problem of looking back. I do, as I said, think that it's good to have a broad-based course. And critical practice definitely applies to studio arts as much as any expanded fine art field. Broad-based means pluralism. Though I have to say that I do also think lack of medium-specificity endangers those who choose to work in those particular areas.

You mean because they have to then go after that subject area grounding themselves?
I think it depends on what staff you have. We have painting staff coming in and so the students who really want to be painters will be put in that tutor's group. Students will see other staff but those will be their core staff and they will be pushed within painting. The same happens with sculpture.

So in a way you maintain a mix?
Yes. Even with a broad-based course the last thing we want is for loads of students to be just 'dabbling' – it's not a continuous foundation course! Say for example you have someone who wants to use film or photography, there has to be a serious reason and consideration for why they are using that, so that they can contextualise their work.

All of those areas that a student might specialise in have a workshop. We have one in painting, one in printmaking, one in sculpture, one in photography and one in time-based media. Students access all of the technical workshops in the first year and usually by the third year they will be talking about why they are using those skills as well.

Whilst we're talking workshops, do you think it's important that craft-based skills are taught in art schools?
Yes, but it depends what a student wants to do. If someone wants to marble-carve, we can't do that here anymore and so they'd have to go away and do that somewhere else. Same thing goes for dead film skills. If a student wants to know how to cast, you want to get them to learn a technique that is up to the level that the technique is at now. If students want to learn particular skills that we don't provide, we try and help them source the best place to do so.

Do you think that the decline in the hands-on teaching of craft-based skills in art colleges is mainly an economic, periodic or pedagogic thing?
It's all of those really. We used to have a bronze-casting workshop down in the basement that most students would use once during their induction and then never again. The same happened when I was at Chelsea in the late seventies.

There are artists now like Anish Kapoor, who don't make their own work. Kapoor for example doesn't make his own sculptures; instead he draws up plans for them and takes them elsewhere to be made. Saying that, Michelangelo had assistants too so it's not just something that happens now.

Also students aren't coming in as skilled.

I wish I could say something about the new course here …

It's also about intellectual input. Art isn't just about process. We can all go down and make a lovely little bronze figurine if we're taught the skill, but what's going on there, where is the enquiry? Maybe that's me making value judgments. Anyway yes, we *are* here as makers as well as thinkers but there are artists who don't end up making anything as there are just too many things to think about!

Arguably a reason that a lot of people come to art college is because they enjoy making things and that's what they've seen art as up until that point ...
Absolutely.

It is really important to just create something. If you haven't done it for a while you miss not having done it.

It makes you wonder if learning about art beyond craft is a progression or a challenge to people's values.
For me, there's no art beyond craft or craft beyond art – just critical practice, intelligent and stupid. It takes all sorts.

Why did you decide to teach?
I was thinking about that today actually. I guess for financial reasons and also because I quite enjoy it. I first started teaching up in Ipswich and I really liked seeing students develop.

Did you do a teacher training course?
No, no, no! I think because I'd been teaching for such a long time I didn't have to do it. But I think if you come into teaching now you have to.

Can art be taught?
I've got to say yes here, haven't I?! Sorry, James Elkins! [Art historian and critic.]

I think you can be shown certain things, yes. When I went to do my foundation I thought all I'd do is draw pictures but then I went on to study sculpture at Chelsea. Art education can open things up and enable you to develop your work. You can also be shown other artists and how you can use their ideas to develop.

Where on the course does the education take place?
We try to get lots of staff teaching in the studios. I think that the more students see staff giving tutorials and talking about ideas, the more they overhear conversations, the better. I was recently talking through critical texts with my sculpture students. We do this in the studios so that other students who are working there, yet not in the class are still listening and therefore in a way, participating. I see education happening here through forms of *action*. There's always something happening and always some active education going on. It's the thing that's seeable, visible, knowable and students take action when they're listening in, moving around with a piece of work or standing back from a painting.

Also, we have film club, art societies, trips, exchanges and private view groups here. We are trying to get students doing things and seeing things. Another action is going out to the pub and sitting down and talking about what they've seen. Seriously! Like with Q-Art, students are coming to that and there's a community of action going on there as they're connecting with students from other colleges.

You mentioned right at the beginning of this interview that it is important that the course modules work in the right way. Can you talk about the unique modular structure of the course and why this is different to other fine art courses?
I'm not really sure it's unique, at all. The same modular structure is something common to all of London Met's BA degrees. I don't think that makes what's taught any different to other art schools, anyway. I suppose there are the so-called learning outcomes: you will have learned this and this and this by the end of this module, and so on. That's no bad thing. The modular structure means I have to think about learning sequence, too, that sort of thing. And modules carry credits, which can be moved to other colleges, if a student really has to leave. So that's good.

Do you have crits here?
Yes we have big seminar crits. For instance, the sculpture or painting groups have big seminars together and then individual tutorials.

And an art history component?
Yes we do. We have a great contextual studies thread running through the BA course.

How many students do you have on the course?
Coming up to 300 now.

Can you identify any differences between art school when you studied and art school now?
You see staff now!

(Both laugh)

I'm serious, it's very different. Joking aside, we never had crits and tutorials with our staff, we honestly never saw them. In fact, they seemed to be a little afraid of students and didn't want to engage with them. Now staff do want to engage, they really do and you can just see them sitting and talking to students. Our students get a hell of a lot of pastoral care. Students all have documentation like these module booklets *(picks up a booklet to show me)*, which map everything that is going on in the year, whereas back then we never knew what was happening. In three years you might move to another room. It was criminal.

Some people argue that there was more creativity going on then or whatever; I can't say. There are more students in art college now, many more students who want to be artists.

You mean people are focussed on that as a goal?
Yes absolutely. What with the Turner Prize and all of that, it's very cool to be involved in the art scene. Cass is in such a fantastic area too and Whitechapel and Shoreditch are places that have changed dramatically because of artists. It's a bit like Soho in New York. Artists bring an energy to an area.

I wonder if the government is thinking about that fact as they cut arts funding?
I don't think they care do they?

Were you on the protest march by the way?
No because I was teaching, but a lot of our students were there. We had a sit in in the North Campus though.

Do you agree with the protests?
Yes. I don't know if I should say that? Well yes I can because you see although it is about the universities, it's not just that because it goes to the heart of our party politics. I think a lot of students feel betrayed because of the Liberal Democrats. I was always Labour but these students have been sold down the Swannee for the Liberal Democrats…and we all thought they were never going to get in but here we are.

Anyway, it's a completely different time. Students now have to fight for themselves, for the next generation and just to 'be' at college – at college where everything's going to be cut back anyway. Either that or they just won't be able to afford to be here.

On the whole I come from quite an apathetic generation. This is really the first time I've seen everyone in my generation get up and stand together to fight for something. There's a huge amount of energy.
Absolutely.

In the 1980s I used to get most of my exercise by marching to get the troops out of Northern Ireland; for anti-apartheid; for the miners' strike and so on. It was great and to be honest also a bit of a social event really. You'd go out, meet friends, go for a long walk around London and feel pretty good about it afterwards. But yes you're right; I haven't seen students do this for a long time!

I come from a generation that entered into adult life in the early Thatcher era. You were either a student that left college to go on and earn a huge amount of money in the city or you didn't earn anything. There were loads of marches going on then. It's good for us to remind ourselves that we have a voice and so we should go out and use it!

Things often happen when you have a government that is trying to squeeze you. People go out and make things happen, especially in the arts, where a kind of freedom comes in. Damien Hirst's auction selling diamond-encrusted skulls to the Russian oligarchs was kind of the end of the Brit Art market boom era. There's a new thing coming along now, well beyond this relational aesthetics thing and there's some really interesting stuff going on in that.

People have been working together, becoming more of a community ...
Absolutely and it's not a put down to do that any more.

Lots of art organisations are working together too. Q-Art for instance, recently teamed up with some others to put on events.
Well as the government is saying, "Up yours *arts*", that does in a sense offer up a certain freedom of thinking doesn't it? Any assumptions of, "Well, we'll just get public funding to do this thing," have gone and so there is a chance for people to think up other models. Of course with all of these shops closing down you have got lots of ready-made gallery spaces ...

Pop-up galleries?
Yes. Councils know that art actually can re-generate an area and so they're happy having artists in the empty shop fronts.

Did you hear about some of the teach-ins at the National Gallery and the Tate?
Yes, though again I couldn't go as I was teaching here. Patrick Brill was there though addressing the crowds and he said it was very exciting. I'll point him out in a minute in the studios – he's great at talking to the students here; he's very sharp and funny.

I couldn't make the Tate sit-in, but somebody there told me that there was a feeling of, "We had our education for free, so let's teach others for free now," amongst staff who attended. True or not, this couldn't really happen now could it?
I don't know how long it would last now but people just want to have the experience of art school – a good one.

Education is amazing and Blair's thing of getting 50 per cent of kids into university *does* also keep people off of the streets, give them opportunity to be away from their parents, away from home and it allows them to get a different view of the world. I suppose in that sense it's a bit like National Service. Only you're paying for it!

Education shouldn't be seen as something for the privileged. It's fantastic that we can all go to university and the more the merrier I think. Let's think about some of the estates in Hackney. The kids on those haven't got a hope. What I mean is that they *hadn't* got a hope and now they've got *even less* of a hope! We've got a government that's ruled by incredibly rich people making decisions for incredibly poor people and I don't think that they could ever empathise. They talk about 'Big Society'. What does that mean? The empty opposite of Thatcher's 'no such thing'.

Changing the subject, what process do you use when evaluating a 'good' work of art, and how does that process differ between here and a gallery space?

It's like you've trained your eye. Sometimes you might get it wrong because conceptually the work means something different from what it looks like, or there are other rules being broken that you had to understand before you came to the work perhaps. I think art college trains you to look at things differently, not differently in a bad way but differently in a way that, say something that might've looked grotesque to you last year, is actually now a very powerful piece to you because you've developed a sensitivity for looking at work.

It's not about like or dislike, it's whether I actually think it's a good piece of work or not, it's the integrity of the work. It's a difficult one to define. There are things that are about certain tastes that you've grown up with and have always worked with. We train our art students to think that even if it isn't to their tastes, they can still look at a work and appreciate the integrity of the work and its qualities.

I see.

I was talking to a student today who likes to play games within her work. I was saying to her that if someone came in and looked at it today they wouldn't get that from it because she's gone for a completely different aesthetic, which conjures a different narrative and causes her work to say something else. I said to her that if she'd titled it in a way to suggest the game within the work then we would look at it again in a completely different way.

I think it's important that we don't deny what the artist is trying to say, however at the same time, once you've made the piece of work it is then the property of the public and the public will come bringing all kind of associations to the piece. Say you thought an artwork was amazing and then you found out that the artist meant something completely different to what you thought it was about. Would that make the work any less good or any better to you?

Good question. One more from me: why do you have a degree show?
Students have worked hard for three years and it is a chance to have a glass of wine and celebrate that. First years don't often get to see the third years' work and vice-versa and so it is also seeing the work of others, putting work up for their peers to see and also a chance to bring Mum and Dad in, especially as in many cases it's them who've paid for it!

The public is also invited in, as are galleries who come in to see what they've been doing. People come in and buy work too.

We are just about to have our Christmas Cookie show this evening actually. You are more than welcome to stay.

STEPHEN CARTER

....

Stephen Carter is the former co-director of Fine Art and a current Fine
Art pathway leader at Byam Shaw School of Art, now part of Central Saint
Martins College of Art and Design, University of the Arts London.
We met in his office in January 2011.

....

Can you outline your position at the college?
Yes. To give an overview: the undergraduate course at Central Saint Martins is very large, it has about 200 students per stage. There is a director
of the overall fine art course – Jane Lee – and then there are the four individual pathway leaders. The fine art course pathways are 2D, 3D, 4D and
XD and my role is to manage the XD pathway, which is about 25 per cent
of the whole undergraduate course.

What is XD?
XD refers to cross-disciplinary practice. Students on this pathway have a
particular interest in testing their ideas across media boundaries. So their
work might move from photography, to painting, to drawing, to performance, to sculpture to installation and so on. A typical student might say for
instance, "these are my concerns" – say it's the human body – and then, "I
want to investigate them through painting, performance, film, text" and
whatever else. What tends to come first with our students are the issues
that they want to discover and then after that the media through which to
approach or discover those issues.

Do students opt for their respective pathways or are they placed by staff?
This will be negotiated.

To give an outline of the other pathways: 2D could be painting, photography, digital imaging, print, the construction of an image and so on. The concerns in 3D are around sculpture, three-dimensional practice and construction. 4D is all about time-based work like film or performance. Most of the course, say 80 per cent, is making compared to 20 per cent theory.

How long have you been teaching on the course for?
I have to give you a complicated answer here. Because one thing has morphed into another, this is my first year of this *particular* job. If you had come 12 months ago I would have been co-director of what was then the Byam Shaw School of Art undergraduate fine art course – the course that has now become a part of Central Saint Martins' BA Fine Art degree. So the short answer is that this is my first year, I'm a new boy. However, the longer answer taking into account both courses, is probably I think about four or five years.

What did you do before?
Throughout my entire professional career, I have refused to teach full-time. Currently I am point six, which means that 60 per cent of my time goes into delivering this course and the rest of my time is at my disposal – I use this for painting and exhibiting.

Does the University support that?
Yes, the University has an allowance for this kind of research. I think many people in this university think it's to the advantage of the student body that the people teaching them are involved in their own practice, dealing with all the difficulties of making and showing work.

Did you study art yourself?
Yes.

Where was that?
I did a one-year foundation course at Canterbury College of Art, which is now part of the University of the Creative Arts. I then did my undergraduate and postgraduate study at Birmingham College of Art and Design, now called Birmingham City University.

Can you tell me all you know about the history of Byam Shaw?
It's actually celebrating its 100-year history. There has recently been a very interesting exhibition at the Lethaby Gallery in Southampton Row, a gallery within Central Saint Martins, to coincide with this centenary. The exhibition, conceived as a celebration, exhibited the work of three artists: two who were originally involved with the foundation of the art school and one, a fairly recent alumni and celebrated artist, Yinka Shonibare. It also looked at the history of the school.

My personal history with the school goes back a long way, I would put it at 1987. I was at a point where even though I didn't want my whole life to be taken over by working in institutions of higher education, I realised that I'd got children and that doing some part-time teaching and selling some work here and there, wasn't a dependable enough income. I don't mind skating on thin ice myself but I don't want to do that for my children. I saw an advert in the Guardian for a job at this place I'd never heard of called the Byam Shaw School of Art, which at the time was based in Fulham and Notting Hill Gate. I applied for the job and I got it.

In 1988 the buildings that Byam Shaw occupied were sold and the School moved to where it is now in Archway. Byam Shaw was a very successful art college at that time for attracting a lot of students and so the reason for the move was primarily to provide more space for studios and so on.

Since that time I've seen some real difficulties and all sorts of changes happening. The school as an independent school, like so many others, could not maintain itself in the contemporary environment and was in effect absorbed by Central Saint Martins and the University of the Arts London. Now, that happened, I think, not because University of the Arts London is a predator – as some people seem to think it is – it happened because this small school needed to be part of a much bigger operation in order to survive.

Do you mean survive in terms of economic or other reasons?
I think economic reasons but also to survive in the global economy of HE that we're now in as well. Of course, things are now changing all over again with our lovely new government and we'll come to see how their massive changes will effect us, our education, and the arts generally.

You're not a conservative voter then?
I'm not getting political but I'm obviously not enthusiastic about what I see coming out of this government and you wouldn't expect me, or any-body like me, to be enthusiastic about it!

So the important thing for institutions like ours and for our students is to ensure that we've got into as good a place as we possibly can be in order to weather the storms to come; and I do actually feel that we've got into that place. There's been a lot of restructuring in recent years and although it hasn't been without pain, I think it has probably put our students and us into the strongest position we can possibly be in.

Last year there was a sit-in?
Yes.

Can you say a bit about that?
I can. Though this is just my version, if you were to talk to some of the students that were around then or other members of staff, they might say something different.

Anyway, I think it was a year ago and it was a reaction to the changes that were happening.

A small institution like the Byam Shaw School of Art attracts a lot of affection, for good reasons. I personally think we were doing a very, very good job. A lot of the things that were happening in that period were very, very good and it's not just me who thinks that; people who know a lot about art and art education agreed and we were getting a lot of accolades from a lot of quarters. So Byam Shaw was in a very strong position academically, artistically and in terms of the respect and affection that there was from students and staff. Given that situation, given that change was coming, and given that a lot of people are apprehensive about change anyway, it was inevitably going to hurt. People were aware that there were going to be cuts, that there was going to have to be a change of culture in many respects, and I think it's very understandable that some people reacted against that and were frightened of it. On top of that there's a kind of sense that a lot of people feel 'small is better'.

I personally respected the people who did what they did in that sit-in but at the same time I think of myself as being a realist and my job meant that I interpreted it rather differently and I wanted to keep communicating with everybody. It's very important to keep the communication channels going. My job was to advise people that in my opinion it was not viable to say "we don't want this". It was much, much better to engage with the process and to make sure that things that we thought were really good about what happens here were transferred to the new situation and that we really understood what we were fighting for. We should not in my opinion, get too sentimental and fight about something that has passed its sell by date and can't survive. So from my point of view I tried to strip away what I considered to be the sentimental aspect of it and put in a hard realism that we wanted to take the things that we were doing that were outstandingly good, forward into the new situation.

Is everything now going to move to Kings Cross, Central Saint Martins' new building?
Not all of the decisions have been finally made, however I do know that the Charing Cross Road and Southampton Row sites will go and everything that's currently happening there will happen on the new Kings Cross site as of Autumn 2011. Blimey, that's not far away when you say it out loud!

The Archway site here will remain and it will be a centre for fine art. I don't think that final decisions have been made exactly as to what goes where and how things are structured but our space is obviously very valuable and it will get used. Whether it's going to be used for MA level work, undergraduate level work or whether we might for example have Stage 1 at Kings Cross and Stage 2 here, these things have not yet been decided. What we do know though is that Kings Cross is going to be the centre and it's going to be very impressive.

Do you have a widening participation programme?
Yes we do. As long as I've been at Byam Shaw, there has been a very strong feeling here amongst myself and my colleagues about the importance of social mobility. It has been a commitment for a long time and it continues to be.

Do you think that the successes of that commitment will be affected by the approaching fee increase?
I think so. Obviously what the government does is going to affect us and we can't escape that. However, I think we as a college, and the University as a university, are absolutely committed to making our education available to people from low income families and that will continue to be the case.

When you were a student did you pay fees?
No. We had no fees when I was a student.

What are the similarities and differences between when you were at art school and art education today?
Gosh! A big question. I suppose economically I could escape leaving with any debts by working every holiday. During winter breaks I worked at the Post Office, riding around on a bicycle, delivering parcels for Christmas and so on. I also sometimes worked all night in a railway station: the night train would come in with the parcels and we'd off-load them, put them onto trucks and off they'd go to the Royal Mail centres.

When I was studying the average student would probably only have to work in the holidays, not term time, leaving them a fantastic five-day week to take advantage of their opportunity to make art and attend lectures. Obviously now there are some well-healed students whose parents might really help them out, but my overall perception is that the average student does have to have work whilst they're studying and they will have to leave with a great debt from their course – both of which are a great shame I believe. Those economic differences have a knock-on-effect on the work.

I think the other big changes are educational changes and I think from that point of view the situation here and probably at other places too is actually better now than it was when I studied.

How so?
What I'm about to say now is a bit of a generalisation but I think it's broadly speaking true. There was a culture of artists and art historians would think, "Oh I'll go and try a bit of teaching." They got work because either they were a talented artist, somebody thought they were a talented artist, or they were on the scene and knew people who could get them that work. Not always but often, their commitment to teaching and their interest in education, in how people learn, was actually quite minimal. I can actually remember times when I first started teaching, when the people who I was working with would make what I consider to be the most ap-palling comments!

They'd say for example, "That work is shit sonny," without any explanation of why they thought it was shit or what about it was good or bad! There was also, "David is a genius!" Where did that come from? Those kinds of pronouncements are completely unacceptable from an educational point of view. What is the student going to learn from getting praise or criticism of that kind? Probably nothing. In fact it could do the reverse and actually damage people. So that kind of irresponsible, egotistical, and not really teaching but opinion spreading, is really thank goodness a thing of the past. There are now education courses etc right across the HE and Art and Design sector for staff like myself that help us to think about how people learn and how we might become a more sensitive teacher.

The University also has in place a training programme where we learn for instance good practice in things like writing reports. I remember times when I used to teach, not here, and students would show me this scrawl that they couldn't even read! What use is that educationally, to not even be able to read what the person is saying? It's rubbish! That kind of thing is also thankfully now a thing of the past. Changes have occurred and the average student now will get intelligent, legible, constructive and thoughtful feedback from their tutor about their practice, their essays and so on.

All of these things are very positive changes. Another thing that's changed is the stuff going on outside of the institution, such as the way that London for example has become such a powerful centre for art. We now have two Tate Galleries, we have all sorts of funded galleries making very good shows and offering educational programmes, there are hundreds of commercial galleries morphing and changing all the time, there are lectures, talks and so much that our students can go to. London is such a stimulating centre now. All of that has had a very positive effect and certainly our position has strengthened partly I think as a result of London's visibility as a cultural centre. Many of our students are attracted here form overseas. They've heard about Central Saint Martins and are also attracted to London as an exciting artistic capital.

Do you encourage students to see a lot of exhibitions?
Yes.

And do you think that they gain a lot of influence from them?
Oh very much so, yes.

Is that a good thing?
Yes. We can be critical or very positive about certain things but in order to do that they have to be aware of things. We're not, and nor should we want to be, immune to what's going on in the big wide world. We're not in the Shetland Islands, we're in London!

There is always lots of discussion about the provision of instructional craft-based workshops within art education. Can I ask how much provision of this kind there was when you were at art school?
My foundation course was very structured but the undergraduate and postgraduate courses I did were both very much conducted in the manner of laissez-faire – there was very little in the way of a definite structure and the staff could be very selective about the students that they took. The idea was that they would take in crème de la crème students in the first place; then get talented artists to come in and then they would basically go around and tell people what they thought. That was more or less it. It's not to say that there wasn't technical staff that could teach somebody to do this that or the other; there was all that, but if a student went or didn't go, there would be no consequence.

The teaching of craft is always an issue and questions over what's the best way of dealing with it get discussed and discussed and discussed.

Sorry to discuss it again!

It is an issue that won't go away. And it won't go away because regardless of what you're making or what medium you're working in it's always there, even with the side that's about ideas, breaking the rules or deskilling. Those latter ideas are quite sophisticated and in order, say, to deskill, you've got to know the skills you are deskilling from in the first place! So it's always an issue. In this university we have a lot of technical resource areas and these areas are filled with technical staff that are very au fait with that particular area of work. Currently what we do is we run inductions in stage one. It is mandatory that students go through these, partly for health and safety reasons and partly to enable them to go back to those areas in order to up-skill should they need to – and that they do via their own initiative. That's how it works at the moment but everything associated with that question is constantly under review.

Would you say that Byam Shaw has a 'thinking through making' or a 'making through thinking' ethos?

In a way there are two answers to that question, one relating to the undergraduate course as a whole and another to the XD pathway within that course. The relationship between making and thinking on all courses certainly needs to be a dynamic one and how that relationship is posited and expressed might change from pathway to pathway and also from time to time. I think we've all seen the situation where a student thinks themselves out of doing anything and nobody believes that that is a good thing.

We've just completed a very interesting unit called 'The Logistics of Practice', which foregrounds the need for ethical practice. We get the students in that unit to ask, "How do we evaluate art?" We get them to come to think about how there might be an aesthetic evaluation, a "This looks better than that," or, "I like how this makes me feel?" kind of thing, and an ethical evaluation. For instance, when we see Sunflower Seeds in the Turbine Hall at the Tate, our reaction might be, "Gross!" That's not an aesthetic but an ethical response; we find it perhaps ethically untenable that one artist should put their name on the labour of a thousand or more people. That's just one example. Ethical issues are in fact attached to every single art practice.

Can you elaborate?
OK, so say you're using acrylic paints, they are a bi-product of the oil industry. The oil industry created the catastrophe in the gulf that affected all of those poor sea birds and all of those people who depend on fishing as a livelihood. Whatever mediums they're working in, we have been stressing how the logistics of ethical practice might impact upon their work.

Now at that point of course you get some students thinking, "Oh dear me, I've never thought about that point before so I'm going to stop doing it." Similarly, you get another student who thinks, "I'm not doing any work any more because I'm thinking about these ethical questions." Now, in a way they're a good student because they're thinking deeply and seriously about some important questions, however, in another way they are a rubbish student because they're not doing anything in an art college where it's all about 'thinking and making' and 'making and thinking'. So these problems constantly come up.

On the other hand you've got a student who's a very good student because they're making things all of the time, but then again they're a bad student because they've not thought at all about these ethical questions or any others in relation to what they're doing!

So our job is to put forward these kinds of questions in order to get people thinking. But we have to make sure that we do so in a way that energises rather than stops their making.

There is that kind of paralysis about isn't there?
There can be yes. It's about achieving a balance.

Has this always been the case or is it a recent thing?
I think that it is probably only a minority of people that get into that situation but ever since I've been teaching and even when I was studying there are always a few that do. They get into a rut of not doing anything because they are 'thinking so hard' or 'reading so much'. In the long run that might be fine because on an undergraduate course like ours, not everyone is going to end up being an artist practitioner. Some people will perhaps end up writing about art, working as a curator, working with a gallery or doing any of the other 101 things that people might do relating to art – and that's not a bad thing.

So in that sense art education can provide a good general education?
Yeah exactly. So it's not bad thing if a person discovers they don't want to be an artist but instead want to be involved in art in a different way.

Can you assess this 'different way' if students discover it mid-course?
It is usually best that the student completes their undergraduate course as a broad platform for their future direction.

Do you think that those students who have not grown up seeing contemporary art are at any kind of disadvantage when it comes to participating in crits on the course?
We are very mindful of a question like this and everyone involved in the interview selection process for new students has to go through university training called 'Fairness in Selecting Students'. The training is very interesting and one of the many things that come up in that process is that we do not want to privilege people at interview stage who might have say had more 'culture' around them when growing up. So we do not want to privilege those who are naturally more familiar with galleries, museums, art of the present and art of the past, than those who've grown up in a less

advantaged background. It's important to stress that this difference in cultural upbringing doesn't mean to say that they're not interested; they are. The policies and strategies that we have in place mean that as far as possible we take students on merit of their potential rather than on what they've been able to achieve to date because perhaps they've been in a more or less advantaged place before they come here.

How do you spot potential?
In a way, when we interview students we're not interested in their portfolio at all. For one that's all history and for two, we're not buying their work, we're not a gallery that wants to put it on the walls! Instead what we're interested in is the work that they will be producing in three years time, how we think they'll respond to the course and how the course will help develop their practice. We are interested in the portfolio from the perspective that it's a very important indicator of their energy, skill and motivational levels, as well as their desire to push on. We're buying futures.

How do people learn to 'read' art and how do you yourself judge a work of art?
That's a big question. Let's start with the first bit: how do we read art?
 I suppose we learn to read art in the way that we learn to read any kind of language – by practising it. I think I'd say that it's a never-ending process; certainly I'm still learning, unlearning and re-learning ways of looking at and interpreting things. Also, I think often it's by exploring the things that appear to be on the edge. For instance, if we understand that there is a thing that we call fine art, then there might be the question "Where does fine art end and something else begin?" So …

(He points to a cup that I'm drinking from)

… Is that a coffee cup or is it art? It's about exploring things that have fallen off of the edge for one reason or another and that's something that never stops. Also, certain principles, like the ethical issues I just mentioned, might cut across each other. For instance, there are entirely different apparatus applied to the evaluation of what art *is*, its ethics, how *good* the art is or isn't, and these are all in turn different from an aesthetic evaluation. Then of course there isn't just one understanding of aesthetics, there are at least three.

So how does the teaching of all that come about in your course?
In a variety of ways. What's important to note is that students usually have very strong opinions and direction in their work when they arrive on the course and they're already engaged in the process of looking and evaluating. Our job therefore is not to introduce those sorts of things to them, but rather it is to challenge their assumptions, to extend their range of looking, to question and argue with them, to introduce them to things they might not have considered before and to deepen their relationship with that process.

Do you think art is a subject that can be taught?
Yes I do. Given what I've just said, I feel quite convinced in my own mind that a student who has completed three years on a course like our one, leaves with more knowledge, more skills, more awareness of themselves, and a deeper relationship with the subject.

Does pedagogy alter with the times? Is 'alter' here synonymous with 'progress?'
It does ...
    Changes are not always 'progressive'.

(He points to a map of Europe on the wall next to where I'm sitting and we both stand up to look at it.)

… Today I met with new students from other parts of Europe who are coming here to study with us as part of the Erasmus scheme. How art is taught changes over time as well as geographically. The way in which art colleges in Athens or Berlin or Paris or Brussels or Amsterdam and so on approach the subject, may well be quite different.

I suppose that the differences all boil down to how different places and colleges structure their art education. This morning a student who studied abroad quite recently was telling me about a system they saw of 'If a student turns up they turn up and if they don't, they don't.' They can simply do another year should they fail. The student and the professor have 'chats' once a week and in order to have the chat the student would turn up on a Monday at say two o'clock to the professor's space – where the professor has got his own practice going on – and on the door that day it might say either, "Welcome, come in," or there might be a notice on the door saying, "Sorry, gone to New York," and so there's no chat that week.

Just like that?
Just like that. The other extreme of course are places where a student is given a timetable that is absolutely regimented, so they know that they're learning *this* on a Monday morning, *this* on a Tuesday afternoon, and that there's *this* lecture on a Wednesday evening – and so on.

So there are huge differences, all based on different ideas of how you teach this subject called art. One is that you learn via the master who does *his* practice – and normally it is a *he* – and has *his* shows, does *his* thing and you learn at the feet of the master, you little person you! Another idea that goes back to Modernism and De Stijl and so on is you *can* structure and teach art.

That model I just mentioned to you just now about the 'chats' might sound like a shambles but I know for a fact that some very good results have come out of that institution. Some people though might question what the hell they're doing there and think, "Well I might as well go and do business studies, this is completely self-indulgent and pointless!"

MARTIN NEWTH

Martin Newth is both the undergraduate Fine Art programme director
and the BA (Hons) Photography course leader at Camberwell
College of Arts, part of University of the Arts London.
We met in the photography studios at Camberwell in April 2011.

*Can you tell me a bit about your position and how long you have been working
at Camberwell for?*
I have two positions. I have been course leader for BA Photography at
Camberwell for the last four years and for the last year and a bit I've also
been programme director for all of the fine art subjects. At Camberwell we
have four fine art subjects: painting, drawing, photography and sculpture.

What did you do before you worked here?
I lectured at various colleges, I was a practising artist – I still am, I did
lots of residencies and I tried to show my work as much as possible. I also
worked for an artist studios group called ACAVA (Association for Cultural
Advancement through Visual Art) as a digital arts trainer. We used to drive
around in a 'Cyber Van' – the 'C-Van', which had computers in the back,
and we did projects with young people on estates. They got to make films
and things and we did that all over London.

Did you study art yourself?
Yes. I did a painting degree at Newcastle University and then I did MA
Fine Art Media at the Slade.

Did you do any formal teacher training?
Yes. When I got the job running the photography course here I was doing a postgraduate Certificate in Learning and Teaching in Higher Education in Art and Design. That was with the Centre for Learning and Teaching in Art and Design (CLTAD). I did that with people from University of the Arts London and the Royal College of Art.

Is it now a requirement for staff to have one of these certificates?
It's not really a requirement yet actually but I think new job descriptions for lecturing posts say that you should either have a teaching qualification or be willing to undertake one. Everyone expected them to become a requirement but it doesn't seem to have ever kicked in.

What was your experience like of doing one? Did you learn a lot? Do you think they are a good thing?
Well you learn most from actually teaching and the course doesn't tell you how to conduct a lecture or anything like that as it's not that kind of course. The training is more about providing a chance to think about different aspects of teaching; to consider the bigger picture and the politics of education. It's also useful to be able to discuss stuff with other staff from different places. You do what is called an Action Research Project, whereby you propose a bit of research in order to find something out about teaching and you test it out in a live teaching environment. I did mine here and based it around how students use studio space, which was very interesting to me.

What made you decide to teach?
I always knew it was something I wanted to do. When I was doing my MA at the Slade I organised a thing with a group of other students called 'Doing Time', which was an exhibition and discussion platform around

the idea of time. We invited all sorts of people into the discussion including artists, architects from the Bartlett School of Architecture, palaeontologists and geologists. I was really interested in accessing all of this fantastic knowledge.

Also, whilst on the MA I did some teaching at the Arts Institute at Bournemouth where I did my foundation course and enjoyed that. I really enjoy teaching and find it a fantastically rewarding thing to do.

Do you think that art can be taught?
Yes! Though it seems that that question is only ever asked about art and not other subjects. If you asked if English Literature can be taught the response would be, "You study some texts, you think about them and you discuss them. That doesn't necessarily make you a good writer but it can help if you want to develop your writing". It's the same with art. We set up the circumstances whereby students can learn loads and take advantage of opportunities for actively engaging with the subject. Through doing that they are being encouraged to make art. So it's setting up the space in order that those things can be possible.

Can you talk a bit about why Camberwell still retains distinct courses for painting, drawing, sculpture and photography?
Yes, absolutely. We made a very specific decision here at Camberwell to not run a generic fine art course and to retain subject disciplines. People apply here to do painting, sculpture, drawing or photography, they don't apply here to do a fine art course and get put into pathways from that. The courses here are separate and I'm fantastically interested in that at the moment.

So I'll start the wrong way around by telling you what our philosophy isn't. It isn't about just trying to hold on to the traditions of a medium or way of working. It's much more about providing students with a centre of gravity, a context and a real focus towards what they're exploring.

In fine art at the moment there's lots of talk about interdisciplinary or cross-disciplinary practice, which is really interesting. However, my point of view is that you can't really have cross-disciplinarity without disciplinarity first.

So it gives students something to start with, understand and hold on to. Also, regardless of whether you're starting art education at 18 or if you're a mature student, I think that an 'absolutely anything is possible, go and be an artist' approach may be too much to grapple with. So contrary to what people might think, I believe that our students end up being less limited. It may seem like quite an old-fashioned way of doing things but students often really kick against and go beyond the boundaries of the discipline, and that's encouraged and made possible by the way we approach the subjects. An interesting observation is that some of the most interesting artists, whose work is cross-disciplinary, identify their practice within a medium even though they may not make work in that medium. For example, Christian Boltanski calls himself a painter and I believe Bruce Nauman refers to himself as a sculptor.

So whilst it's quite at odds with most other institutions, it provides students with a distinct choice about why they come here. And philosophically, I think we have the right approach at the moment.

Are there points when everyone comes together?
Yes. So whilst students on each course do a series of contextual studies courses relative to their subject discipline, there are also a series of lectures and debates that get students up to speed with key vocabulary and ideas, for example, post-modernism or an introduction to aesthetics that are relevant to anyone engaging with fine art generally.

There are also cross course crits, and artist talks every three weeks whereby we try and pick artists whose work is cross-disciplinary. In the second year, when the students get back from Easter, all the fine art students do an exhibition together. All of these are about exploring the expanded notion of what your practice might be as well as what happens when someone who calls themselves a sculptor works next to someone making a painting or something else.

Within the different courses, is there any provision for taught skills?
Yes, absolutely. And that's something that's really helped by having a subject specific approach. If you have a generic fine art course and a series of taught workshops, the list of what you might do is endless, whereas having subjects makes that list more manageable.

So within photography for example, there are clearly skills that one needs in order to operate the equipment and make work. We have a menu of workshops, delivered by technicians, that students can sign up to. There are all sorts of sessions from working in the black and white and colour darkrooms to working with a digital camera and shooting in the studio. We also have artist-led workshops whereby either a member of staff or an artist we bring in will deliver a two-day, ideas or approach-led workshop. We don't run workshops like this to say "everyone must take this approach or idea and use it", we run them in order to open up to students the possibilities for working in certain ways.

To give an example, we recently ran a workshop on the constructed image. That was both an approach to making work and also involved using the studio and lighting in a particular way. We're developing these workshops on the other courses as well. For example, in painting we also currently run a series of painting technology and surfaces workshops.

So workshops are something I'm particularly interested in. I think they are as important as theory, as important as doing crits and as important as discussing work. Making art, as anyone who's made any knows, is all about juggling all of those different bits. It's also for us about getting the balance right to make that happen. When you ask students what they want many of them say that they want skills-based teaching all of the time. I do not think that the attitude of hoping students will just 'pick it up as they go along', which is what my educational experience was like, is appropriate or right.

Changing the subject slightly. Do you know what is happening with the foundation course here and across the University of the Arts London?

The three foundation courses from Camberwell, Chelsea and Wimbledon are being amalgamated into one in order to form the CCW Foundation, which will be based in Wilson Road, Camberwell. The overall number of students isn't going down that much and so the course will retain something like 750 places. Applications for the course have been fantastically high and students really want to go there. I think it's going to be an amazing course and it's in a brilliant building – a Victorian school with lots of space. Wimbledon College of Art are selling their current foundation building, so for them it must feel like something is disappearing but it won't affect any current students as the foundation course is only a year long and so all of the new students will be at Wilson Road.

May I ask you about the college's widening participation policy?

Well the policy is that widening participation is something we really focus on at the University. It is something that we are always encouraged to think about and there's a section where we have to write about it in our annual course monitoring report. At Camberwell we're particularly open to the possibility of people coming here from a diverse set of backgrounds. I think we're perfectly situated to do that better than other places in London because of our location and because of the fact you can live in this part of London reasonably affordably compared to the places where the other colleges are. Our portfolio of courses – lots of design and art courses – also attracts a more diverse body of students and we're trying to do more and more work going out to local colleges and schools to encourage people who may not have thought of applying to art school, to come to Camberwell.

Are you going to be running a socially engaged practice module here?

Yes. We're going to have a unit called Socially Engaged Practice and Collaboration.

We are currently re-validating our courses – which means that we're re-writing our course handbooks – and for lots of reasons it's really important that we make clear what our focus is as an institution, relative to others. Of course in the age of £9,000 fees and prospective students shopping around, making a clear and distinct offer is imperative. So our single disciplines are key to this, as is our location, and our location lends itself to an enquiry about what socially engaged practice might be.

Recently we had a debate here called 'What is socially engaged practice?' and the fact that that is a question is key. The term has a currency in contemporary art and has some baggage with it. There is a sort of expectancy by some people that socially engaged practice means that you set up a kind of market stall affair and make badges. That might be one way of having a socially engaged practice but it's certainly not the only way; there are lots of different possibilities. We're interested in getting our students to ask what socially engaged practice might be. The second years will do a collaborative show around January or February, there will be a series of lectures, debates and seminars around associated ideas and then they'll be asked to generate their own collaborative projects, which could be an event, an exhibition or a screening. A very key part of a student's experience at Camberwell will be whether they either take on board or reject ideas of social engagement and what that might mean for them.

This element of the course also has links with Peckham Space. Peckham Space, in Peckham Square, is part of Camberwell College of Arts and commissions work that explores possibilities for art that is socially engaged and is made in partnership with the community. It seems appropriate that people understand the relation between what we do in the art college and what Peckham Space does.

Will the module run across all of the courses?
Yes and it will be interesting how that is negotiated and grappled with. I think with most photographic practices you need to have at least asked how you engage in a social context, whereas there is a notion that paint-

ing is a lot more private and internal. There are though fantastic examples of artists that make objects or paintings and who also have a politically or socially engaged agenda in their work.

Is Camberwell unique in offering this course?
I don't know. We've decided it's something we're going to focus on and it feels right. I don't mind if other people are going to be doing it, as there are examples of similar courses that have been incredibly successful. The environmental art course at Glasgow had Douglas Gordon, David Shrigley and a whole raft of people that became very well known. There must be other examples of courses taking these ideas on board.

You mentioned earlier that there are both course crits and cross-course crits. Are these led at all?
Yes. We have a member of staff, sometimes two, leading reasonably small groups of about 12 or 15 in crits that last half a day. When I started teaching, crits used to last the whole day but that seemed to be less and less popular with students.

But I think your question is about students leading stuff. Another big ambition of mine, and I've discussed this with staff of similar ambition, is that we set up a situation whereby students can be guided towards research interest groups that they identify with. So say a student is interested in Feminism and they're in sculpture or drawing, there will be a platform to develop, read-around and discuss those ideas within a student led, cross-course interest group.

That does sound very interesting. I think my question though was more, if the crits are as you mentioned led by staff, how do the staff lead them?
What does the member of staff do?

Yes.

Oh OK, yes. The key thing I think for the member of staff, is to describe at the start of the session what the session is. People assume that in art schools students know how to behave in a crit but it's not a natural thing to do actually, it's very unnatural. So I think it's about setting it up and it's important to change the way that crits are done every time. For example, in the last one we did, everyone was invited to talk about the work in the crit before the student showing the work said anything. The showing student would then respond to what was being said.

I think that the staff's role is to keep the conversation moving appropriately and to pick up on and encourage development of what they feel are the most pertinent points that have been made. This is in order that the student whose work is being discussed is helped as much as possible in that scenario. It's very important to have members of staff there but then again the worst crits are where the member of staff does most of the talking. The point is for the students to discuss work and that unexpected points can be raised and move the discussion forward.

You said how being in a crit situation is not actually a natural thing to do. This made me think. A crit situation is about looking at and 'reading' someone else's work in order to discuss it and offer feedback. How do students learn how to read work? Is that a taught skill or is it picked up through being in that situation?

Well you get better at it the more you do and we also run sessions on reading and discussing work. So in one of these sessions we might have loads of images on the wall that don't have any title or artists' names and students have to try and work out what's going on in that work. We then look at whether the titles match or change the way they think about the work. It's about honing skills and allowing people to become more sensitive to the way work might operate.

It's also about confidence. I've often got much better things to say about work the day after and it's fine realising that but I think with confidence you get a bit quicker. I also think that one of the most valuable things about being in the environment of the art school is that you can make mistakes in front of your peers. You can say the wrong thing or make bad work and feel OK about it. In some groups it happens naturally and in others it takes a lot of work to make people feel comfortable to say things they're not quite sure about.

There has been a lot of commentary in the likes of Art Monthly on the current assessment culture and it has often been suggested that students do not feel free to take risks anymore. Do you think that this is true and that assessments do weigh heavily on students?
It's a massive question this one. Assessment may weigh down on students but if it does they're putting the pressure on themselves. Students really want to be assessed.

There is one theory that the clearer, the more rigorous, and actually the more often people are assessed, the more likely assessment is to go to the back of their minds. Rote learning – where people learn facts for the sake of it without actually understanding what's behind them – is seen in our country as less preferential to a type of education that is more about developing ideas and understanding things. But research has suggested that those people who just learn stuff actually have as much, if not more potential to develop creatively because that stuff 'just exists'. So then the idea that making assessment more frequent means that it becomes less significant, makes sense. Assessment really is not that important and so it's about making students aware of what's going on and making them not worry about it. But however much we tell them so, it's still very important to them that they are being assessed.

In a way we're getting them too late to change that attitude because they've been brought up having been tested since they were five. A friend of my daughter who is four has just had an entrance exam for a school and I couldn't believe it!

She's four?
Yes!

(Both laugh)

This is the world we live in.

But, importantly, it is possible to build things like 'risk-taking' into the assessment.

Can you tell me about any differences between art education when you studied and art education now?
Yes. So I studied at Newcastle University between 1992-1996 and at the Slade between 1997-1999. The situation has changed entirely. At Newcastle University it was more like being on an artist residency than having the kind of educational experience that exists now. I'm not knocking those who taught me there because they were fantastic people, but there was very little sense that there was any kind of structure to our experience. We were given very large studio spaces and a few bits of equipment and we just went in and made bits of work. Now and again someone would pop in and have a chat with us and even that got less frequent the further up the course you got.

A few people are still making work and did well from that experience, but it was all about your staying power and self-confidence. It wasn't really about anything else, which in my view was not the perfect situation.

So whilst you can hardly open a book or a magazine about art without reading about 'the death of art education', I am absolutely convinced that the experience we give to our students now is many times superior to the one I got. They get much more from it, they understand much more the context within which they're working theoretically and I believe they make more informed work and are slightly sharper. So despite the fact that everyone says it's the opposite – that art education is getting worse and worse

– even on my pessimistic days when I think that might be true, I remind myself that somehow the work seems to get a bit better every year. So, for me, it's not all doom and gloom.

Do you think that the rise in paper work and student numbers is part of making a better student experience for more people or do you think it is frustrating?
Firstly, it's true to say that art schools could have been better run since they've been changed but a change *was* required. The people that write about how art education has completely gone to pot are probably fantastic artists who have a lot to offer but may not actually be very suited to being educators and don't want to see that as their role. They see their role as an artist who will influence the generation behind them and I just don't see that as a very interesting approach. Some artists seem to think that art schools owe them a living in some way and often I get the sense that the people writing very negative things about art schools are those individuals.

So there is lots of paper work but I feel that that came about partly because the structures weren't sound or enough. The structures that were in place weren't properly thought out and were structures for their own sake.

Not everyone will agree with me but I think that you have to have lots of really watertight structures in place in order that you can forget about them. It goes back to that assessment thing I mentioned. If the timetable is completely rigorous and assessment procedures are tied up and all of those things are completely clear and structured, then students can forget about them and do the interesting stuff, which is talking about ideas and making art.

I also don't agree that the rise in student numbers is a bad thing. Obviously there is the impact on space but for me that's the only real limitation. On the photography course we've had rising student numbers and whilst yes you get more students, you also get more *good* students and that allows the conversations to be broader.

This is not to say everything is fine and rosy, everything isn't fine. The government has decided not to take higher education seriously and we are being asked to do more and more. Everything has got to be about employability and not about the quality of the experience and it seems absolutely extraordinary that they've decided to withdraw funding from the very thing that's been most successful in the last twenty years.

Do you think that the £9,000 tuition fees that University of the Arts London has decided to charge students from 2012 will deter students, or less well off students from applying?
Yes, I'm really worried it will.

Do you know what measures the University will put in place to attract students from lower income backgrounds?
We don't know exactly what the measures will be yet. The University made the argument to charge an extra £400 per student, above the £8,600 it was calculated that it would be necessary to charge just to break even in London. That put the price up to £9,000 so that we could afford to develop as a university and offer more bursaries. But it is deeply disturbing for me. The idea that art somehow returns to being privileged people making work for privileged people is not very interesting at all.

Students have been critiqued for entering their degrees with an expectation or concern for a career – perhaps as a consequence of the fees...?
It's not just because of fees. It's another interesting problem that art schools and all education has to deal with. In a way there are two ways of thinking about what a degree in art might offer. One is that it should offer protection and a space to develop, think and make mistakes; that it should provide this protective cocoon in which to create. That was a bit like my art education. Another attitude is that it should give students experience of what it's going to be like to work after they leave and make them really grapple with some of the mechanisms and functions of the world out there.

Each institution has to decide I think which one of those it does. We've decided to give students lots of experience of writing proposals, putting on shows and engaging with the real world outside. There is an argument against that which is that it's going to stifle any risk-taking and will make people ultra aware of the products they're producing. It is a danger but I think as long as we're aware of it we can stop that happening. I think you can have a situation where students are engaging with the outside world as well as really questioning, developing ideas and taking chances.

Is the art market the only example of how an artist might continue their practice post-art education?
No. There are loads of examples of other ways of operating. I think it's really important that you show these to students and so we invite in lots of artists who aren't just showing in West End galleries. We also have people who have been to art school and now work in other creative spheres that come in to talk to our students as well.

You didn't pay fees did you?
No. I think I was in the last year when you could still get a grant to do an MA, which I got. There were only a few colleges in London that you could apply to for an MA where you could get a grant and I think they were Chelsea, the Royal College of Art and the Slade. If you wanted to go to Goldsmiths or Central Saint Martins you didn't get a grant, which meant that I only applied for the three!

I think the biggest impact of the fees now will be on the MAs because if you've accrued £30,000 or more worth of debt during your BA, you're much less likely to take on an MA and two more years of debt. That's going to seem less and less attractive I think.

Presumably those fees will increase as well?
They already have and will increase more. I think ours will be £6,000 next year.

Did you grow up seeing contemporary art?
What a brilliant question. Absolutely not. There was a really notable and quick change between the time when I began studying art and just two years after. At the beginning of the nineties there seemed to be almost no awareness of contemporary art at all and then almost overnight it was everywhere. So when I was a foundation student, contemporary art was Lucian Freud and Francis Bacon. Two years later it was Damien Hirst and Sarah Lucas. It also became better known within the public psyche and the Turner Prize also got more people aware of it.

That awareness brought about loads of brilliant things but it also in retrospect had a detrimental affect on British Art. The whole Brit Art thing could be blamed for a lot. It was about one person collecting work and so it was down to one person's particular taste and that person came form advertising. What that meant was that work had to be quick, it had to be easily digestible and it was often accompanied by a little blurb, like an advertising tag line. At the same time the word 'curator', which originally means 'to care for', seemed to change its meaning. It was all about these people as well as the public, understanding stuff incredibly quickly.

What that meant was that the idea of making work that involved set-ting up something really difficult and challenging for the viewer, which I feel is the most interesting kind of art, was put to one side for a bit. Most art became quick and easy and so art students, instead of thinking 'I really want to enter art school because I want to explore something and find something out', saw that that you might be able put a couple of objects together, paint them orange, get a snappy title and there's a bit of Brit Art. It also had to be sellable and it was all about the market. All of the other functions of art seemed to get marginalised for those big sexy things and that was bad.

Do you think that students are still influenced by the market now?
Yes but I think what they've also got now are loads of different ways of operating to choose from and things like a more socially engaged practice are very visible. It's a much more exciting place to be now where there are these different models but no hierarchy in terms of ways of operating. It means that there are less art stars as well. In the nineties there seemed to be about 20 artists that everyone could name whereas now there are loads of people, all very interesting, very different and all very high in profile.

Do you think that reputations of art colleges influence students?
I was thinking about this the other day. When I applied to go to the Slade it seemed that places had a clear identity. You knew you would get a very different experience from going to the Slade than you would the Royal College of Art. There was the perception for example, that if you applied to Goldsmiths you'd be buying into Michael Craig Martin and Brit Art. If you wanted to go to the Royal College it was about honing your skills. The Slade was about tearing apart and rebuilding your presumptions and ways of making, and at that time it felt there that there was a greater emphasis on materials.

I expect anyone who works in these places may hate me saying this because they've probably worked so hard to dismiss all of this.

I think a lot of institutions have become very aware of the negative aspects of having a 'house style' and so I think places have become more similar. Staff have also moved around institutions. So whilst less 'house style' is good because it isn't interesting, there is something to be said about having distinct offers from places. I personally think that something interesting comes out of an argument as opposed to a polite conversation. So a college that says "This is where we stand. Agree with us or take us on," can be a good thing.

So, perhaps the only good thing about this fees thing is that with students shopping around, institutions have got to make it clear what it is they're offering.

How do you select students?

It's an incredibly rigorous process. We do it on a portfolio, a personal statement and on the photography course we ask people the same six questions. What we're looking for is people who know why they want to study, why they've chosen this course and that they can show in their work already that they're interested in developing ideas. We're not interested in final products, rather the potential to investigate.

What does art education offer?

It's a really fantastic experience and I don't think you should ever test its success on how many people end up being artists or end up being in the Turner Prize because it can be an extremely positive experience in so many different ways. Hopefully, it gives students confidence in their ability to research, articulate ideas and start to understand the world. For these reasons, going back to your question about selecting students, I would go with Joseph Beuys and let everyone in!

POSTSCRIPT:

....

As I was writing this book I had an email from someone who had found out about Q-Art. They told me that they would be coming to our events because they cannot afford to go to university for their art education.

....